Meditations for Women Who Do Too Much

Other Books by Anne Wilson Schaef, Ph.D.

Women's Reality

Co-Dependence: Misunderstood, Mistreated

When Society Becomes an Addict

The Addictive Organization (with Diane Fassel)

Escape from Intimacy

MEDITATIONS
FOR·WOMEN WHO DO TOO MUCH

Anne Wilson Schaef, Ph.D.

HarperSanFrancisco
An Imprint of HarperCollinsPublishers

Credits are listed following the index.

HarperCollins Web Site:
http://www.harpercollins.com

HarperCollins®, 📖®, and HarperSanFranciso™
are trademarks of HarperCollins Publishers Inc.

FIRST HARPERCOLLINS PAPERBACK EDITION
PUBLISHED IN 1990

FIRST HARPERCOLLINS MASS MARKET
PAPERBACK EDITION PUBLISHED IN 1996
ISBN 0–06–251437–7

An Earlier Edition of This Book
Was Cataloged as Follows:

Library of Congress Cataloging-in-Publication Data
Schaef, Anne Wilson.
Meditations for women who do too much
/Anne Wilson Schaef.—1st ed.
ISBN 0–06–254866–2 (pbk.)
1. Women—Prayer-books and devotions—
English. 2. Devotional calendars. I. Title.
BV4527.S27 1990   89–45960
242'.643—dc20

96 97 98 99 00 ❖ OPM 10 9 8 7 6 5 4 3 2 1

ACKNOWLEDGMENTS

I want to thank so many people who have helped bring this book into being. Let me thank first of all, my agent, Jonathon Lazear, who called one day and said, "I have just sold a book you didn't know you were writing." "Oh no you haven't," I fired back. Then we discussed it. Jan Johnson at Harper and Row was very convincing, and I remembered that way down deep I had wanted to write a meditation book years ago. I also have finally come to believe that I am a writer and I was ready to "try my wings" on some challenges. So I said yes. I loved the process, and I thank Jan and Jonathon for challenging me.

Then there are the people who backed me up. Diane Fassel and John Reed at home gave me constant support and feedback and helped gather quotes. Linda Lewis worked hard to gather excellent quotes. Mary Ann Wells, Linda Crowder, and Gwen DeCino typed and put things together. Ann Sprague did the tedious, time-consuming, and very important work of checking the quotes, checking the typing, making content and editorial changes (as well as great personal comments, such as "I like this one," "Ugh," and so on), and generally whipped the book into shape. My grown-up kids and son-in-law added the needed peppering of encouragement.

We made a great team, and I am more and more convinced that no book ever comes into being through the efforts of only one person. I have had a wonderful time working on this book. It has stretched me as a writer, organizer, and thinker. Perhaps we will do a sequel for women who are *recovering* from doing too much. Who knows?

Most of all, I want to thank the wonderful women whose quotes and lives make up the substance of this book and the Twelve Step Program of Alcoholics Anonymous, without which the clarity for this book would never have been possible.

INTRODUCTION

This is a meditation book for women who do too much. When my publishers first suggested doing this book, we talked of the need for a book for women workaholics. Yet, as we discussed the need for such a book, we began to explore the many different kinds of women who overwork and do too much and agreed that many of us would not initially define ourselves as workaholics. However, there are many of us who do too much, keep too busy, spend all our time taking care of others and, in general do not take care of ourselves. Many of us have crossed over the line to compulsive, addictive, self-defeating behavior and need to make some major changes in our lives. Hence, I decided to write a book for women who do too much regardless of where we do it or how we do it. This is a book for women workaholics, busyaholics, rushaholics, and careaholics. I hope that it will prove interesting, challenging, and helpful to a range of women.

I decided to use only quotes from women. This does not mean that there are no tempting, exciting, and useable quotes from men—there are. However, I found so many wonderful quotes from women that I decided to use them exclusively. I have used a variety of quotes from women. I have tried to use quotes from women of different ages, cultures, disciplines, and perspectives. I have used quotes from famous women, women at intensives, and women who just said something important in passing. This gathering of women's quotes has proved to be a rich and enriching experience for me.

In preparation for this book, I returned to several novels by and about women that I had read in the sixties and seventies. What a wonderful rediscovery! I met old friends (the heroines) who had rested dormant in my soul and again came alive as I returned to them.

Some of them re-emerge on these pages. I hope you enjoy them as much as I did.

This book of meditations is not only for women, even though it is written from a woman's perspective, in the female idiom and is viewed through the eyes of women. Several men have read the manuscript and found it very helpful. I am happy to share these meditations with anyone who finds them useful. I know that there are many of us who are working ourselves to death and still not making our contribution. Life does not have to be that way.

In some ways this book follows a usual form for meditations and in others not. There is a meditation for each day of the year. Each day begins with a quotation, which is followed by a meditation on it, and ends with a few words for the day. Since I assumed women who do too much would not take much time for meditations (and probably usually take none!), I tried to make each meditation brief. In addition, I have added several "extra" meditations at the end of the book. If you do not respond to one on a particular day, look at one of the extras.

These meditations do not tell you what to do, they do not tell you how you should be, and they are not answers. They are intended to stir up some feelings, get you thinking, and precipitate possibilities for change which will add to the quality and vitality of your life. These meditations can be experienced as an open door or a direct hit to the solar plexus. Make of them what you will.

RUSHING/FRENZY

Anything worth doing is worth doing frantically.
—New proverb

We women who do too much find the ending of an old year and the beginning of a new year to be a difficult time. There is always the temptation to try to "tidy up" all our loose ends as the old year closes. We fall into the trap of believing that it is possible to get our entire life "caught up" before starting a new year, and we are determined to do it.

Also, there is the temptation to set up an elaborate set of resolutions for the coming year so that we can, at last, *get it right*. As workaholics, we tend to be very hard on ourselves: nothing less than perfection is enough. Hopefully, on this first day of the year, we will be able to remember that we are perfect just as we are.

I HOPE *for the willingness to live this year in a way that will be gentle to myself . . . one day at a time.*

POWERLESSNESS

We are powerless over our workaholism and our busy-ness, and our lives have become unmanageable.
—Modified Step One, Alcoholics Anonymous

Me? Powerless? No, never! The very word causes me to curl my lips and to have grave suspicions of any creature who would suggest it. As a woman, I will never be powerless again. I may be expected to be, but I won't be!

But wait a minute. This step does not say that I am powerless as a human being. It clearly states that I am powerless over my workaholism and my busyness. Now that's a different matter. I have indeed felt a little ragged around the edges, and I am concerned that my relationships and other aspects of my personal life have been taking a beating lately.

Even when I try to stop, I find I can't really. Maybe I need to be willing to take a look at this "powerless-over" idea. My life does need something.

JUST BEING WILLING *to take a look is the first step. I can take that step.*

January 3

EXCUSES/CHOICES

*So at an early age I witnessed the fact that work was
of the first importance, and that it justified rather inhuman behavior.*

—May Sarton

Workaholism, just like other addictions, is intergenerational. Many of us have learned it at home from our
mothers and fathers, and we cannot even imagine any
other way of being in this world. Work took prece-
dence over everything in our households and families.
We could only have fun after the work was done, and
the work was never done. We could only relax and
take care of our personal needs when the chores were
completed and the house had been straightened up.
And when that was done, we were much too tired to
do anything else. Cleanliness was always next to godliness, and many times godliness seemed very far away.

Work was always tied to the necessities of life, getting ahead, and the American dream, and these ideals
justified anything, even cruel and inhuman behavior
in the family.

We learned our lessons well, and now we have the
opportunity to break the intergenerational chain of
workaholism. We have a chance to be different. We
have choices.

LET ME NOTICE *today how many times I use work
as an excuse for my inhuman behavior.*

HUMOR

Time wounds all heels.

—Jane Ace

We lose the ability to laugh *at* ourselves and *with* others.

Humor is so healing . . . and it's fun too. We find that humor is one of the first human gifts to disappear when addictive diseases set in.

We lose the ability to laugh *at* ourselves and *with* others. We feel insulted if someone pokes fun at us, and we personalize everything, seeing it as a put down. The more our disease progresses, we make Scrooge look like a stand-up comic. Indeed, instead of being heal*ers* we have become heels . . . heels without souls.

Good humor is very inexpensive. It is one of the pleasures in life that is relatively free. I'm sure, if we try hard enough, we can remember a part of us that used to laugh and be playful.

———————————

HUMOR *doesn't die, thank goodness, it just goes underground sometimes and digs caverns for our "serious" selves to cave in to.*

CRISIS/EXHAUSTION/CONTROL

The sky is falling! The sky is falling!
                                        —Chicken Little

Living our lives like Chicken Little can be quite exhausting. Yet so many of us live from one crisis to another! We have become so accustomed to crisis and deadlines that we feel almost lost if we are not putting out some kind of fire. In fact, if we really were honest, there is something dramatic and exciting about handling a crisis. It makes us feel as if we have some modicum of control in our lives.

We have, however, on occasion wondered if all these crises are normal and if there is another way to live life that might be a little less exhausting. Even though we are exhilarated in handling these crises, they do leave us feeling drained. Could it be that these things don't just *happen* to us? That we have a hand in their creation?

As we begin to work on our recovery, we see others around us who do not live from one crisis to another, and they seem to do just fine . . . they're even serene.

CRISIS and my illusion of control are not unrelated. I hope I will allow myself to be open to noticing the relationship between the two in my life today.

SELF-DECEPTION/ILLUSIONS

We live in a system built on illusions and when we put forth our own perceptions, we're told we don't understand reality. When reality is illusion and illusion is reality, it's no wonder we feel crazy.
—Anne Wilson Schaef

All addictions are built on illusions. The illusion of control, the illusion of perfectionism, the illusion of objectivity. Dishonesty and denial are the building blocks of addiction. When we participate in any of these illusions, we are deceiving ourselves, and when we deceive ourselves, we lose ourselves. Why is it that we find self-deception and illusions so much more attractive than honesty? It could possibly be because we are surrounded by a society where illusion is the name of the game. Denial runs rampant at every level of our society, and there is not much support for "truth speakers."

Yet, we are the only ones who can deceive ourselves. We are the only ones who can refuse to acknowledge our perceptions and lie to ourselves. The choice to deceive ourselves is ours.

———————

THERE IS *an old saying, "Conscience is a cur that will let you get past it but that you cannot keep from barking." Sometimes our awareness makes funny noises to get our attention.*

RIGIDITY

*Changes [in life] are not only possible and predict-
able, but to deny them is to be an accomplice to one's
own unnecessary vegetation.*

—Gail Sheehy

Part of the crazy thinking of addictions is that we will
be safe if we can just get everything in order, everything in place, and keep it that way. Much of our energy is spent trying to contribute to the calcification
of our lives. Unfortunately, calcified beings are brittle
and break easily.

When we become rigid about anything, we lose
touch with our life process and place ourselves outside of the stream of life—we die. As Lillian Smith
says, "when you stop learning, stop listening, stop
looking and asking questions, always new questions,
then it is time to die."

HAVE I *already died? Am I one of the walking dead?
Rigid isn't stable, it's just brittle.*

NEED TO ACHIEVE

Some of us are becoming the men we wanted to marry.
——Gloria Steinem

Getting an important position in a good company is an exacting feat. Many of us have worked long and hard to get where we are and we are proud of our achievements.

Success demands sacrifice and focus, and we have learned how to do both. We have put our work before everything else in our life. We have learned to compete and compromise. We have learned to dress like men and hold our own in a circle of men. We have learned to be tough and to "come on strong" when we need to. We wanted to make it in a man's world, and we have. We have learned to play the game.

It is time to stop and see what has happened to us in this process. Are we the *women* we want to be?

———————————

I WONDER *if I have really become the man I would want to marry? Would my clear and healthy woman want to marry me?*

ANGER

Anger as soon is fed as dead
'Tis starving makes it fat.

—Emily Dickinson

Anger has not been an easy emotion for us. We get angry when we are passed over for promotions. We get angry when no one listens. We get angry when our ideas are not heard and even angrier when these same ideas are declared "fantastic" when one of our male colleagues presents them. We get angry when we are so strung out and exhausted that we find ourselves yelling at those we love the most. Then we become angry about being angry, and we try to "control ourselves."

It is important to remember that feelings are just that . . . feelings. It is normal for us to have feelings, and it is normal for us to feel anger. Anger is only harmful when it is held in and "starved" as Emily Dickinson says. When we hold it in, it builds and we find ourselves exploding on innocent people in the most astounding circumstances. Then we end up feeling bad about ourselves and getting anger backlash from others. We need to find safe places to let our anger out. We can respect our anger. It is our friend. It lets us know when something is wrong.

ANGER *is not the problem. What I do with it is.*

Juggling Projects/Negativism

I don't give myself credit for what I do get done because I have so many projects hanging fire that I haven't done.

—Chris

We workaholics are the type of people that see a glass half-empty instead of half-full. It is much easier to see what we haven't done than it is to see what we have done.

Often, if we just stop and take stock, we have really accomplished quite a bit. In fact, we probably have been a wee bit close to the edge of working wonders.

Unfortunately, we miss the opportunity to marvel at our wonders because we have so much set up still to do that what we have done pales into insignificance in relation to what is (always!) yet to be done. Ugly is in the eye of the beholder.

———————————

TODAY *is awareness day for what I have accomplished. Celebrations may be in order.*

CHANGE/SECURITY

People change and forget to tell each other.
—Lillian Hellman

How tenaciously we cling to the illusion that we will get our lives in order and they will stay that way! How resistant we are to the normal process of change! We often feel personally attacked if someone near and dear to us changes without clearing those changes with us first. We have somehow come to believe that security and stasis are synonymous.

Change is the manifestation of our ability to grow and become. When it occurs in those nearest and dearest to us it is an opportunity for celebration. When it happens in ourselves, it allows us to share ourselves on a new level. When we try to protect others from the awareness of our changes, we are being dishonest. No one can care for who we are unless they *know* who we are.

———————

THE ONLY *constant is change.*

CHOICES

To gain that which is worth having, it may be necessary to lose everything else.
—Bernadette Devlin

Sometimes we become very dramatic with our lives and believe that if we are to get what we want, we have to sacrifice everything that is near and dear to us. The "excellence" books tell us that if we want to get to the top, we have to be willing to sacrifice spouse, children (having children), hobbies, and anything in our lives that is not related to work in order to "make it." Some of us have tried to do that. We have become workaholics and in that process lost ourselves. Without ourselves, we ultimately have little or nothing to offer. We have tried to shut out our need for closeness, friendship, rest, and leisure, believing in the rightness and nobility of our decision.

We have sacrificed for our work. We have fulfilled the romantic dream of giving our all. We have excelled.

IT IS NEVER *too late to re-examine our choices. Re-examination is wise. We always have choices.*

COMPASSION/RUTHLESSNESS

*And beyond even self-doubt no writer can justify ruth-
lessness for the sake of his work, because being human
to the fullest possible extent is what his work demands
of him.*

——May Sarton

What May Sarton has written is not just true for a
writer. No one can justify ruthlessness!

We are told that one has to be ruthless to make it in
the world of business. As women, we have believed
that we have to be even more ruthless than men just
because we are women. Many of us have achieved success, but at what price? We don't like who we see in
the mirror.

One of the characteristics of the addictive process is
that we progressively lose touch with our own morality and our own spirituality. We progressively lose
touch with our humanness. Recovery affords us the
possibility of reconnecting with our compassionate
self.

———————————

MY ABILITY *to be compassionate and experience the
beauty of my humanness has not left me. It was only
buried under layers of addictive garbage.*

January 14

BELIEF

*Why indeed must "God" be a noun? Why not a verb
. . . the most active and dynamic of all?*
                                                —Mary Daly

Some of us have difficulty with the concept of God
because we have seen God evolve into something or
someone who is static, a mega-controller, and frankly
someone who is not that nice to be around. Traditionally, we have tried to make God static so we would
feel safe. That is our problem, not God's.

What if we see God as a process—the process of
the universe? What if we begin to understand that we
are part of the process of the universe? What if we realize that it is only when we live who we are that we
have the option of being one with that process? Trying
to be someone else, who we *think* we should be, or
who *others* think we should be, ruptures our oneness
with that process.

———————————

IF GOD *is a process and I am a process, we have something in common with which to begin.*

GIFTS

Make good use of bad rubbish.
                              —Elizabeth Beresford

It's really up to us what we do with our lives. We may have been battered, beaten, molested, incested, spoiled, or over-indulged. All of us have feelings and memories we need to work through. None of us had perfect families. In fact, dysfunctional families are the norm for the society.

The question for us is how have our experiences affected us and what do we need to do to learn from our experiences, to work through those lessons, integrate them into our being, turn them over, and move on?

When we get stuck in our blame, anger, hurt, and denial, we are the ones who suffer. It is up to us to "make good use of bad rubbish."

―――――――――――――

IF MY LIFE *resembles a garbage dump, it is up to me to sort it through, turn over the soil, and plant flowers to make use of all the natural fertilizer.*

FREEDOM

Learning moment by moment to be free in our minds and hearts, we make freedom possible for everyone the world over.

—Sonia Johnson

Freedom begins within. Addictions are the antithesis of freedom. By definition, addictions are anything that have control of our lives and are progressive and fatal. Being addicted to doing too much is no different from being addicted to alcohol or drugs. We are hooked, and we can die from these workaholic behaviors.

Freedom from addictions is an important first step toward personal freedom. In Twelve-Step circles we often hear that "These addictive diseases are the only fatal diseases for which recovery is guaranteed if we do our work." When we are addicted, we have lost our minds and hearts to the disease. As we start to work a recovery program, we begin to have a new appreciation of the word *freedom*.

———————————

MY RECOVERY *work affects others, whether I know it or not. Freedom is a possible dream.*

THINKING

To achieve, you need thought. . . . You have to know what you are doing and that's real power.
— Ayn Rand

Thinking sometimes takes a bum rap in some circles, and it is over-exaggerated in others! As a society, we have become so lopsided in rational, logical, and linear thinking that many of us have become confused about the process of thinking. We are very dualistic in our thinking about thinking.

We have come to believe that we must either be cold, calculating, logical, rational women, or we must throw all thinking out the window and carry the load for all the feeling, intuitive aspects of our society. Either of these solutions results in a languishing lopsidedness that leaves us wanting.

There is nothing wrong with thinking. It's the *way* we do it. Often, when we lead with our logical, rational minds, we have not allowed them to be informed by our being and our other thought processes of intuition, attention, and awareness. It is in the synergy among all these aspects of our mind that true thinking begins.

MY BRAIN *is a great gift. Using all of it increases its value.*

LIVING IN THE MOMENT

Love the moment, and the energy of that moment will spread beyond all boundaries.
—Corita Kent

We women who do too much have a terrible time loving the moment. We are always making lists and eyeing the tasks that are just around the corner when we need to be busy working on the task at hand. Hence, rarely does anything get our full, undivided attention. Because of this subtle distractibility and lack of presence, we miss a lot.

When we really can be in the moment, the very process of being in the moment radiates into the crevices of our life and begins to dust out the cobwebby corners.

———————————

PRESENCE *is such a gift . . . to myself and others.*

CONTROL

People who try to boss themselves always want (how-
ever kindly) to boss other people. They always think
they know best and are so stern and resolute about it
they are not very open to new and better ideas.
                                        —Brenda Ueland

We workaholics are difficult to be around. We are hard
to work with and hard to work for. Our core form of
functioning is control. We often do not know the difference between getting the job done and getting the
job done well. Our belief is that if we can just control
everything, we are doing our job and doing it right. Our
illusion of control is killing us. We find ourselves exhausted and burned out.

Unfortunately, control is costly. In trying to realize
this illusion of control, we are destructive to ourselves and others. Also, in trying to maintain this illusionary control, we find our field of vision becomes
more and more constricted (as do our blood vessels!)
and we are no longer open to new and better ideas. In
fact we are not open to any ideas at all.

———————————

WHEN, *in my controlling behavior, I do unto others*
as I do unto myself, we all lose.

CONTROL

She was a "what if" personality and because of that she never really happened.
                                        —Anne Wilson Schaef

We addicts are "if" people. We use our "iffing" to try to control our past, our present, and our future.

If only we had been more assertive, we would have made the promotion. *If only* we had been more intelligent, we would have done a better job.

Our "as iffing" tries to cope with the present. We act *as if* we know what we are doing. We act *as if* we are calm and relaxed. After all, we have developed *some* skills!

Yet it is our "what iffing" that really keeps us paralyzed and feeds our illusion that we are in control. We try to imagine every possible exigency and prepare for it before it happens. If I just cover every base, I will never be caught wanting. My "iffing" has resulted in my never being present to my life.

――――――――――

WHEN I QUIT *"iffing," I may just start living.*

FEAR/DISHONESTY/DENIAL/ CONTROL: STEPS ONE, TWO, AND THREE

The liar in her terror wants to fill up the void with anything. Her lies are a denial of her fear: a way of maintaining control.

—Adrienne Rich

Our fear is like the first tile in a string of dominoes. Our denial of fear causes us to lie, to cheat, and to become people we don't even respect in order to maintain our illusion of control. We lie because we are fearful, and we are fearful because we lie. It is a circular process and we feel stuck in the middle of these raging feelings.

What a relief it is to admit our fears! What a relief it is to admit that we are powerless over our fears and they are making our life unmanageable! This opens the door to admit that if we return to our inner process, our power greater than ourselves, we can feel sane again.

ALL OF US *are afraid sometimes, that's human. When our life is ruled by fear, that's addiction.*

OBSTACLES

In the upper echelons of the corporate world, it helps to be good-looking . . . but only if you're a man. If you're a woman, attractiveness can be a handicap.
—Diane Crenshaw

Sometimes it's difficult to accept that the obstacles in our life are there for a purpose and that we have something to learn from them. Some of the obstacles seem so unfair . . . and they are! There still are many double standards operative in the world of business (and elsewhere!). What works for men often doesn't work for women in the same situation. And it isn't fair . . . true . . . and we resent it . . . right . . . as well we should. And while we are trying to change the situation, it is important to see what we have to learn from these unfair obstacles and move on. We don't like them, and it is up to us what we do with them.

OBSTACLES *often are not personal attacks; they are muscle builders.*

January 23

HONESTY

When a woman tells the truth she is creating the possibility for more truth around her.

—Adrienne Rich

Honesty is contagious, just like dishonesty is contagious. We need more honesty in the world.

Many of us have prided ourselves on being honest. We have always tried to be honest and have believed that we were. It has been frightening when we have been told that we are "too honest," or when we have been told that we will not be able to get ahead if we insist on being so "brutally honest." Slowly we have learned to "compromise." We have learned to say what is expected of us and not to offend. We have lost touch with the awareness that we are being dishonest when we go ahead and agree to do something that we really do not feel right about doing. We have come not to expect honesty from ourselves or from those around us. We are even surprised when we encounter it.

————————

IF WE WANT *to heal, we have to start getting honest with ourselves and others. Creating the possibility for more truth is up to each of us.*

INTIMACY

. . . just a tender sense of my own inner process, that holds something of my connection with the divine.
—Shelley

Intimacy, like charity, begins at home. If we cannot be intimate with ourselves, we have no one to bring to intimacy with another person.

Intimacy with ourselves takes time. We need time for rest, time for walks, time for quiet, and time to tune in to ourselves. We cannot completely fill up our lives with activities and become intimate with ourselves. Nor can we just sit quietly indefinitely and become intimate with ourselves. We have to have the time and energy to *be* our lives and to *do* our lives in order to establish an intimate relationship with ourselves.

Surprisingly, as we become intimate with ourselves, we discover our connection with others and with the divine. Neither is possible without intimacy with ourselves.

―――――――――――――

INTIMACY . . . *In/to/me/see. It won't hurt to try it.*

LETTING GO

When I am all hassled about something, I always stop and ask myself what difference it will make in the evolution of the human species in the next ten million years, and that question always helps me to get back my perspective.

—Anne Wilson Schaef

"Little things mean a lot," especially when we focus all our attention on them, obsess and ruminate about them, and can't let them go. Sometimes, when we are in our disease, we just keep turning disturbing thoughts over and over in our minds, believing that we will surely figure out some solutions if we just think about them long enough and check out every angle.

When we engage in this behavior, it is a sure sign that we are in the addictive process and thinking ourselves to death. I have always found that when I am in my addictive process, I have lost perspective. I suddenly become the center of the universe, and my problems are the only ones in the universe.

It always helps me to step back and realize that whatever problem I am having is probably not of universal proportions. This perspective helps me to see that I am powerless over my crazy thinking, and that it is making my life insane. At this point I can get back in touch with my knowing that a power greater than myself can restore me to sanity, and I can turn this problem over to this greater power.

———————

ONE *of the things we lose in the addictive disease process is perspective.*

FINANCIAL SECURITY

Humans must breathe, but corporations must make money.

—Alice Embee

It's okay to make money. It's even okay for corporations to make money. Unfortunately, money addiction is so rampant in this society that we have lost all perspective on making money. We have become addicted to the *process* of making money. The money itself has become irrelevant. It is the process of accumulation that has us hooked. No matter how much we have, it is never enough. The same is true at a corporate level. More is never enough. We have developed a frantic obsession around accumulation of money. We gather, we spend, and we hoard. We have forgotten that money is not real. It is symbolic. It is legal tender. It is a form of exchange. It has become so real for us that it is more real than our health, our relationships, or our lives. Money addiction and workaholism often go hand in hand.

FINANCIAL SECURITY *is a static concept that is illusionary and expands exponentially as we reach our former static goal.*

FORGIVENESS

It is very easy to forgive others their mistakes. It takes more gut and gumption to forgive them for having witnessed your own.

—Jessamyn West

How we hate to be seen as our most naked selves! We feel noble when we forgive others their awful mistakes, yet we become paralyzed with guilt and shame when we realize that they have caught us in our worst moments. It is so tempting to try to find something wrong with them and take the focus off what we have done. The best defense is a good offense, we have been told. How hard it is to let ourselves claim and own our mistakes! Yet, also how freeing.

We have the possibility of not only forgiving those who have witnessed our mistakes but also of embracing them as a gift to help keep us honest.

———————

SOMETIMES *my gifts are so well-wrapped I have difficulty recognizing them as such. As I unwrap myself, I can unwrap each present.*

EXPENDABLE/CONTROL/FEAR

When I was sixteen, my mother told me that I was expendable and if I didn't work hard, companies could just get rid of me. I work sixty to seventy hours a week, never take time off, and my husband and I haven't had a vacation in twelve years. I'm a workaholic, and I love it.

—Anonymous Woman

Whew! Need I say more? This woman has bought the whole package.

Like her, many of us believe that we can control what we perceive as our expendability by making ourselves indispensable. What a sophisticated illusion of control! Obsessive working is different from a passion for our work.

Usually people who are truly passionate about their work are also passionate about their play and their time for themselves. Workaholics are not. We work out of fear and try to convince ourselves that we love it. Fear and self-abuse go together.

———————————

AM I *expendable to* me? *That's the question.*

POWERLESSNESS: STEP ONE

In the face of an obstacle which is impossible to overcome, stubbornness is stupid.
>   —Simone de Beauvoir

Some of us do not like to hear this, but there are some things in our lives over which we are powerless. In fact, when it comes right down to it, there are few aspects of our lives that we can really *control!*

Certainly the areas of our lives over which we are truly the most powerless are our own addictive, compulsive working, rushing, busyness habits. In fact, that is one of the definitions of addiction. An addiction is anything that controls our lives, over which we are powerless, and which is making our lives unmanageable. Our inability to stop killing ourselves with doing too much certainly fits into this category.

KNOWING *when to quit may be my greatest victory.*

AWARENESS OF SELF

*Human beings are an untidy lot. They'd lose their
arms and legs if they weren't joined on right.*
— Elizabeth Beresford

Our addictive functioning requires of us that we tune
out our bodies. In fact, often the purpose of our addictions is to put us out of touch with what we are
feeling, what we are thinking, our awarenesses, and
our intuition. Addictive working or rushing around
leaves little time or energy to notice what our bodies
are telling us about our feelings and our health.

We have come to think of our bodies as nonexis-
tent and often experience little below our necks.
Some of us even spend most of our time "out of our
bodies." Instead of seeing our bodies as our allies and
sources of important information, we have come to
see them as vehicles for the practice of our addiction,
and we use them as objects. We have forgotten the
way our bodies move and the way they feel moving.

————————————

I BETTER *pay attention to the messages from my
body. If I don't, it will get my attention, perhaps through
extreme and painful measures.*

GIVING OURSELVES AWAY

Somebody almost walked off wid alla my stuff.
— Ntozake Shange

As women, we are often so generous, especially with ourselves, that we give little pieces of ourselves away, to almost anyone who asks. At the time, we hardly notice. Sometimes the pieces we give away are so minuscule that they really seem unimportant . . . a favor here . . . letting something go by that we know is wrong there . . . swallowing the anger from an injustice done to us somewhere else. We can handle each one individually, and we are unaware of the cumulative effect of years of giving away little bits and pieces of ourselves.

We sit up and scream, *"Somebody almost walked off wid alla my stuff!!!"* We have allowed ourselves to be almost devoured by those around us.

———————

GIVING MYSELF AWAY *and being stingy are not my only options. I can share myself. Yet to share myself I have to* have *a self to share.*

FREEDOM

How is my own life-work serving to end these tyrannies, the corrosions of sacred possibility?
—June Jordan

Sometimes, when we stop and reflect, we need to believe that the work we are doing has a meaning beyond the tedium of the everyday. In fact, if we cannot see some larger connection in what we are doing, we often experience a feeling of loss or emptiness.

We know, somewhere deep inside us, that even if *what* we are doing doesn't exactly have a great cosmic meaning, the *way* we go about it and the interactions we have with others around our work can give it meaning beyond itself. Regardless of what we do, we do have an opportunity to make it sacred work.

I ALWAYS *have the freedom for a sacred possibility.*

February 2

HAPPINESS

It is not easy to find happiness in ourselves, and it is not possible to find it elsewhere.
—Agnes Repplier

We are the wellspring of our own happiness. Our happiness resides within us. No one else and nothing else can give it to us. We may try to find all kinds of things outside ourselves to fill us up and make us happy, but they are all short-lived. We think success, recognition, respect, money, and prestige will do it for us. They're nice for a while, *and* the feeling lingers that something is missing. This does not mean that a happy person cannot have all these accouterments of success—she can. Happiness, however, is not a *result* of these symbols of success.

Happiness is ethereal. It only dwells within, and when we seek it, it becomes even more elusive.

I HAVE *the opportunity to open myself to the happiness that is mine today and not try to fill myself with happiness substitutes.*

ALONE TIME

*And when is there time to remember, to sift, to weigh,
to estimate, to total?*

—Tillie Olsen

Such a little thing: finding time alone. We have often felt that if we took time for ourselves, we were taking it away from our children, our spouses, or our work and therefore it must be a perversion.

So many little moments during the day are so precious to us. Those few moments after we have sent everyone else off for the day and we can breathe . . . those times alone in the car or on the bus or subway when no one around knows us or can intrude . . . those sighing times in the bathroom when nobody is there . . . even those stolen moments alone while doing the dishes are precious to us.

———————————

IT'S ALL RIGHT. *Moments alone and our need for them are not a perversion, they are a life-giving force.*

February 4

GIFTS

Problems are messages.

—Shakti Gawain

I always believe that the intensity of the whack alongside the head that life has to give us in order to get a
lesson through to us is directly proportionate to the
height and breadth of our stubbornness and illusion of
control.

Problems give us the opportunity to learn something. If we don't get the learning the first time around,
we get another chance, and another, and another. If we
miss the learning completely the first time, the next
whack will be a little harder, and then the next time
even harder. We get many opportunities to learn the
lessons we need to learn in this life.

Obstacles are gifts for learning. We never really
know what we have learned until we have learned it.
Then we are ready for the next learning.

I HAVE *the opportunity for many gifts today. I hope I
see them.*

EXHAUSTION

Whatever women do they must do twice as well as men to be thought half as good. Luckily, this is not difficult.

—Charlotte Whitton

Although some of us hate to admit it, it is probably true that we "have to do things twice as well as men to be thought half as good." And it is probably also true that we can produce at a level that boggles the mind.

What we tend to ignore is the cost. Working as hard as we do and as long as we do is exhausting. Sometimes we dread becoming aware of how tired we are. Sometimes it almost seems as if the marrow in our bones aches.

Women have a tremendous fear of feeling our tiredness. We are afraid that if we let ourselves feel it, we will never get up again.

MY TIREDNESS *is mine. I have earned it.*

February 6

BELIEF: STEP ELEVEN

Neither reproaches nor encouragements are able to re-
vive a faith that is waning.
———Nathalie Sarraute

Faith, in the last analysis, is a personal process. One of
the problems that we as women face in accessing our
spiritual self is all the things we have been told that we
should believe. We have tried to swallow beliefs from
outside. Rarely have we taken the time and effort to
go inside and start with our own awareness and understanding of God or a power greater than ourselves
and let ourselves trust our own knowing. In our busy
lives, it is easier to reject than "wait with" our knowing. It is easier to move on than it is to "be with."

No one else can give us the answers about our spirituality. Reading and thinking cannot provide the solutions. Our spirituality is experiential, and it is intimately connected with who we are.

———

SOMETIMES BELIEFS *have interfered with my con-*
nection with a power greater than myself. It is time to
"wait with" my knowing.

DEADLINES/STRESS

*Tension grew at home, and my work suffered as I com-
mitted to tighter and tighter deadlines.*
— Ellen Sue Stern

One of the myths about workaholics is that they are
very productive and they do good work. Myths are
confusing because we often act as if they were true,
even when we know that they are not.

Contrary to popular belief, we workaholics and
rushaholics are often not very productive, and we often
do sloppy, uncreative work. Our overextended deadlines become more important than the quality of our
work. We suffer, our work suffers and our families
suffer.

Another myth about workaholism is that it is just
stress and burn-out and can be controlled with stress-
reduction techniques. Every drunk has wanted to blame
something else for her/his drinking and has fervently
wanted to believe there was a way to control it, often
with disastrous results. Workaholism is an addiction.
It is a progressive, fatal disease that rules our lives. Fortunately, an addiction is the only progressive, fatal disease from which recovery is guaranteed if we do our
work.

MAYBE *it is time to check out a Twelve-Step meeting.*

CLARITY

*Well we start out in our lives as little children, full of
light and the clearest vision.*
                                        —Brenda Ueland

When we begin our recovery from our addictive doing-
too-much, we may have little or no experience of
what clarity or sobriety from our addictive behavior is
like. We have muddled around so long in these addictive thinking patterns and behaviors that they almost
seem normal to us. The last time we experienced clarity may well have been when we were children.

After we have admitted our powerlessness over our
addictive, compulsive work behavior, and after we have
begun working the program for a while, we may suddenly have a moment of clarity. It surges through our
consciousness like a meteor and scares us to death. Yet
we sense that whatever we experienced is something of
extraordinary importance. It is like a lullaby sung long
ago. The words are faint, and the melody reverberates
in our being.

CLARITY *is not unfamiliar to us . . . we have just
forgotten what it is like.*

SUCCESS/GRATITUDE/CLIMBING THE LADDER

Though a tree grow ever so high, the falling leaves return to the ground.

—Malay proverb

Many of us work for and aspire to professional success. We have worked hard and long to get where we are, and we deserve the rewards of our position.

It is important that we periodically take time to take stock of *where* we are and *who* we are. Do we judge ourselves by our accomplishments? Does accomplishment mean worthiness in our book? How have we been able to get where we are, and do we feel good about the way we did it? Do we need to make amends to some people and express our gratitude to others?

It is important to recognize that our achievements not only speak well for us, they speak well for those persons and forces, seen, unseen, and unnoticed, that have been active in our lives.

SUCCESS *offers me the opportunity to reflect on those who have given me much and to be grateful for their gifts.*

COMMUNICATION

*Some people talk simply because they think sound is
more manageable than silence.*

—Margaret Halsey

Women who do too much need to keep busy. One of
the ways we keep busy is talking even when we have
nothing to say. It's not that we are so taken with the
sound of our own voices. It is just that silence seems
so overwhelming and murky.

Much of our lives has been spent filling up . . .
overeating and filling up ourselves . . . overworking
and filling up our time . . . overtalking and filling up
our shared moments of silence.

As we begin to recover, we find that we do not
need our "filling-up fixes." We can be with ourselves
in silence.

WHEN PEOPLE TALK *on and on, they usually are
not listening to themselves.*

ACCEPTANCE/CONFLICT/FEELINGS

When Peter left me, the negative emotions that rose up in me and exploded in me were just horrifying. But God kept telling me that they were all part of me and I couldn't try to hide them under the carpet because I didn't like them.

—Eileen Caddy

There are events in the passage of our lives that elicit feelings we never knew were there and of which we believed *we* were completely incapable. A spouse wants a divorce or has an affair. A boss passes us over for someone younger, prettier (we believe), and less-qualified (we know for certain), and we find that the witches of Endor or the dragons of old have nothing on us. We could belch fire and melt diamonds with our breath.

Right, good, so what? It is normal to have feelings like this. It is not healthy to dump them on others or to hold onto them. They will rot inside us.

WHEN I FEEL *these feelings, I have another opportunity to learn something new about myself. Thank you . . . I think.*

GOALS/COMPETITION

What you have become is the price you paid to get what you used to want.
                                    —Mignon McLaughlin

Was it worth it? Is it worth it? Can we look in the mirror and say to the person we see, "You are someone I trust and really admire"?

We must remember that each step along the road of life is like taking a walk. It gets you somewhere, and steps often leave footprints.

We cannot say to ourselves, "Well, what I am doing is expedient now, so I will go ahead and do it this way. I will deal with the consequences later," and not *have* consequences later. The denials of our life are interrelated.

———————

WHAT I DO *becomes who I am. I am working with precious elements here.*

PERSONAL MORALITY

*I cannot and will not cut my conscience to fit this
year's fashions.*
> —Lillian Hellman

One of the effects of the addictive process is that we
gradually lose contact with our personal morality and
we slowly deteriorate as a moral person. It is easy to
see how the alcoholic or drug addict is progressively
willing to lie, cheat, steal, and even kill or hurt the
one she loves in order to get her fix. But women who
do too much are not so different. We have moral slippage too. We will withhold information, lie, mislead,
or undercut others to get ahead. We are willing to
compromise our standards and our morality to get to
the top, to "fit this year's fashions." When we compromise our personal morality, we have sold our souls
and we are losing the "us which is us."

Part of recovery is to recognize that our personal
morality is one of our most precious assets and too
important to treat lightly.

———————————

I VALUE *myself enough to realize that my personal
morality is a beacon that demands to be followed.*

February 14

EXPECTATIONS

Nobody objects to a woman being a good writer or sculptor or geneticist if at the same time she manages to be a good wife, good mother, good-looking, good-tempered, well-groomed and unaggressive.
— Leslie M. McIntyre

Right! So what's the problem? It's not easy to be well-groomed when we have toddlers running around . . . but we try. It's not easy to be good-tempered and un-aggressive when we have deadlines at work and at home . . . but we try. It is not easy to produce children and be svelte and good-looking . . . but we try.

There is probably no group of people in this society who try harder than women to meet the expectations of others. As a result, we are always looking outside for validation, and no matter how much we get, it isn't enough. In always trying to be what others think we should be, we have lost ourselves and end up having little to bring to any relationship or task.

EXPECTATIONS *are like girdles. We probably should have discarded them years ago.*

February 15

FEELING CRAZY

You can't start worrying about what's going to happen. You get spastic enough worrying about what's happening now.

—Lauren Bacall

Why is it that *we* always seem to be the ones that need the help. We do feel crazy at times, and feelings of being overwhelmed are not unfamiliar. And yet, why does the label craziness (if someone has to be crazy!) always rest on us?

Sometimes, it's a relief to admit that we feel crazy. We do need someone to talk with when we feel isolated. Others appear to cope all right. Why can't we? At least, talking with someone or going to a group with other women helps us recognize that we are not alone in these feelings. Seeking out help and support can be a real turning point. Groups for workaholics are, after all, free.

PERHAPS *my inability to cope with an insane situation the way I always used to is a sign of my movement toward health.*

BECOMING/ILLUSIONS

It's our illusions about our illusions that hang us up.
                    —Anne Wilson Schaef

Our addictions lead us into a life of illusion. They feed our illusion of control, our illusion of perfection, and our dishonesty. Our addictive behavior allows us to deny reality and justify not living our life. We slip along in a mist of illusion, whether they be illusions of romance, illusions of power, or illusions of success—and somehow we miss life.

One of the significant qualities of an adult is being able to separate ourselves from illusion and to nourish ourselves with reality, rather than feed on illusion. Contrary to popular opinion this does not mean that we have to live dull and staid lives. It means we have to *live* our lives.

———————————

WHOOPEE! *Let's try reality for a change.*

AWARENESS OF
PROCESS/CONTROL/CREATIVITY

*Living in process is being open to insight and encounter.
Creativity is becoming intensively absorbed in the process and giving it form.*

—Susan Smith

When we choose to live our lives in a process way, we
choose to be open to all that life has to offer. Our illusion of control has often filtered out new insights and
encounters. We have been so focused upon our goals
and the way things *have* to happen, that we have missed
the succulent serendipity of chance awarenesses. We
have been so afraid of losing our illusion of control
that we have missed some of the richest encounters
that life was offering us.

When we can participate fully in the process of our
lives, we discover new forms of our creative self. Creativity has many avenues. Just living our lives can cultivate our conscious creativity.

CAN IT BE? *Is just living my life enough?*

FRANTIC

We have come to a place where frantic and panic seem integral to being a woman, especially a professional woman.

—Anne Wilson Schaef

Women who do too much tend to get frantic over almost anything. Where *did* we park that rental car at the airport and what in the world did it look like anyway? We were *sure* that we parked our own car right in front of the drugstore at the shopping mall. Or was that last week?

Where did we put that bill that simply must be paid today? There must be a way to get the kids off in the morning that could be less frantic. We are *sure* an organized mother could do better.

Where is that pen? Where is that pan? Where are those pants? Probably right where we left them. It is usually our "frantic" that clouds our vision.

FRANTIC AND PANIC *are old familiar friends. Maybe it is time for them to move out from our house.*

JUGGLING PROJECTS

We are traditionally rather proud of ourselves for having slipped creative work in there between the domestic chores and obligations. I'm not sure we deserve such big A-pluses for all that.

—Toni Morrison

Women who work outside the house aren't the only women who are obsessed with work. Women who are home full-time rarely have time for themselves and their creative projects. After all, children are twenty-four hours a day and the house is twenty-four hours a day. There is always something to do.

Our greatest skill is not perhaps in getting things done, it may be in juggling projects so it looks like we are getting things done, so that we feel better. Watch out! Juggling projects is one of the symptoms of the workaholic. Instead of paring down the projects to those that can reasonably be done, the workaholic tries to do it all.

JUGGLERS *aren't paid very well, and sometimes they get hit on the head with balls they have in the air.*

AMENDS

Make it a rule of life never to regret and never look back. Regret is an appalling waste of energy; you can't build on it; it is good only for wallowing in.
—Katherine Mansfield

Looking back and regretting are very different from taking stock, making amends, and moving on. When we look back and regret, we are indulging in the self-centered activity of beating ourselves over the mistakes in our past.

All of us have made mistakes. When we have operated out of the craziness of this addictive disease process, we have done much harm to ourselves and others. We have neglected ourselves. We have neglected those we love. That is the nature of an addiction. Now we can admit our wrongs, make amends to those we have wronged (including amends to ourselves when we have not been caring for ourselves), and move on.

We cannot build on shame, guilt, or regret. We, indeed, can only wallow in them.

———————————

OWNING *and making amends for my mistakes affords me the opportunity to build on my past and integrate it. I can start doing this anytime . . . maybe even today.*

VALUES

When women take on a career, they don't discard their female values, but add them onto the traditional male values of work achievement and career success. As they struggle to fill the demands of both roles, women can't understand why men don't share this dual value system.
—Susan Sturdinent and Gail Donoff

One of the often most painful learnings for women who work outside the home is that the same skills that work in business just do not work in our homes and in our personal relationships. Luckily, we have the advantage of knowing a value system that does contribute to living, and we have only to learn what works at work.

Unfortunately, in the process of learning a career value system, we are encouraged to denigrate our values and sometimes we succumb to this pressure. Our values are not wrong. They are different. And the workplace would be richer with them.

———————

TRUSTING *my value system can be a major contribution to my work.*

SOLITUDE

*"Thrice welcome, friendly Solitude, O let no busy foot
intrude, Nor listening ear be nigh!"*
—from *Ode to Solitude* by Hester Chapone

Solitude is such a blessing! Everyone needs time alone.
Often we are fearful of time alone, because there is no
one for us to encounter but ourselves. How comforting it is to go to ourselves! How much like returning
home to an old friend or lover after having been away
too long visiting places that felt foreign and unfamiliar.

Our solitude is one of the pleasures that only we
can arrange. It is up to us to see that we regenerate
through our time with ourselves. We have the right,
and we have the power. If we do not model respect
for our own need for solitude, our children will never
learn that they deserve their time alone.

———————————

LET ME REMEMBER *that I have the right to create
a space of solitude for myself, if only to enjoy the soothing sound of running water in my own bathtub.*

HONESTY

Lying is done with words and also with silence.
—Adrienne Rich

As we begin to heal, we have a new appreciation of Jesus' words, "You shall know the truth and the truth shall make you free." Part of the purpose of our addictive behavior is to put us out of touch with ourselves, and when we are out of touch with ourselves, we cannot possibly be honest with anyone. We have to know what we think and feel to be honest with others. In our early recovery, we slowly begin to realize how far we have wandered from ourselves . . . a long way, indeed!

We have been fearful of speaking our truth honestly. We have been afraid of losing our jobs, losing our friends, and losing everything we have. Yet, as we become more honest, we begin to untie the tangled knot of dishonesty, self-centeredness, control, and confusion. We see how our dishonesty has led to our confusion and even when it is difficult, we find ourselves sighing in the refreshing breeze of honesty.

I AM SLOWLY *relearning about my ability to be honest. I am astounded with how far I had ranged from myself.*

CHOICES/RESPONSIBILITY

We're swallowed up only when we are willing for it to happen.

—Nathalie Sarraute

When we talk about taking responsibility for our lives, we must clarify what we mean by responsibility. The addictive meaning of the word responsibility means accountability and blame. When women accept that meaning, they cannot bear to take responsibility for their lives or to see other women do so, because, they assume, taking responsibility means taking the *blame* for where they are and who they are. Unfortunately, this attitude puts us in the position of being a victim and robbing us of our power.

It is only when we accept that we do have choices, and we exercise those choices, that we can reclaim our lives. Inherent in this reclaiming process is owning the choices we have made (all of them!) and moving on. Thus we are not blaming ourselves for our lives; we are claiming them and owning them so we can take our next steps.

———————————————

I HAVE MADE *some bad choices, I have made some so-so choices and I have made some good choices. The most important aspect of them is that they are mine— all of them.*

PAIN

*Iron, left in the rain
And fog and dew,
With rust is covered.——Pain
Rusts into beauty too.*

—Mary Carolyn Davies

Our pain is ours. Some of it we have earned, the rest not, and it is still ours. When we fight our pain, we fight the experience of our humanness, and we lose ourselves in the process. A life without pain is a life of nonliving. Our pain lets us know and come to understand the full meaning of being human. If we fight the normal experience of our pain, we lose the possibility of experiencing the process of its rusting "into beauty too."

We don't need to seek pain, but when it is inevitably there, we have the possibility of something new entering our lives.

———————

MY PAIN *is a possibility. It is not a liability or a punishment.*

NURTURING ONESELF

*Just the knowledge that a good book is awaiting one
at the end of a long day makes that day happier.*
— Kathleen Norris

The art of nurturing oneself is not something that is
taught in most high schools or even in a good MBA
(Master of Business Administration) course. In fact,
the art of nurturing oneself is rarely taught in families
either.

Yet, in this high-tech, high-information society,
learning how to nurture oneself is absolutely essential
for survival. Some good workaholics have found that
if they do a cursory job of nurturing themselves, they
can work even harder. Unfortunately, that isn't nurturing oneself, that's protecting one's supply.

Nurturing oneself is allowing ourselves to stop,
and in that stopping to allow ourselves to know what
would be nurturing for us in that time and space, and
doing it.

WHAT IS NURTURING *at one point in our lives
may not be nurturing at another. In order to nurture
myself, I have to know myself each moment.*

PERFECTIONISM

This is the age of perfectionism, kid.
Everybody try their emotional and mental and
*   physical damndest.*
Strive, strive. Correct all defects.
                                            —Judith Guest

Perfectionism is one of the characteristics of addiction. Perfectionism is setting up an abstract, external ideal of what we should be or should be able to do that has little or no relationship to who we are or what we need to do and then trying to mold ourselves into that ideal.

In trying to be the abstract perfect, we batter, judge, and distort ourselves. No matter what we do or how we try to achieve, it is never enough. We are never enough. Trying too hard and never trying at all are two sides of the coin of perfection. Unfortunately, it is a coin that never pays off.

PERFECTIONISM *is self-abuse of the highest order.*

LAUGHTER

Laughter can be more satisfying than honor; more precious than money; more heart-cleansing than prayer.
—Harriet Rochlin

How long has it been since you have had a good belly-laugh? Good laughter seems to be a treasure that is in short supply of late.

Most of us are distrustful and embarrassed by our laughter. As children we were constantly told to suppress it. Often it seems almost lost to us. We are afraid to laugh alone, and we are embarrassed to laugh with others. What a state!

Laughter is one of the gifts of being human. We can't force it, but we can sure stop suppressing it in ourselves and in our children.

———————————

LAUGHTER *is like the human body wagging its tail.*

February 29

IMPRESSION MANAGEMENT

And yet, all these years I'd been terrified I would be stoned to death if people saw through the facade.
— Sara Davidson

How much time and energy we spend in impression management! We firmly believe that if we just dress right others (especially men) will think we are professional, intelligent, competent, and in control. We believe that if we just dress right others (usually men) will think we are attractive, sexy, desirable, and worth knowing. We think that if we are just caring, understanding, and constant enough someone will want to be with us.

We have such terror that someone will see through our facade and discover (our greatest fear!) that no one is there. We believe that if people really know who we are, they would have no interest in us. We believe that it is our impression management that keeps us safe.

———————

OF COURSE, *if someone falls in love with my impression, they aren't loving me, they're only loving my image.*

IN TOUCH WITH
PROCESS GREATER POWER

*We both of us secretly believed in an external power
that one could tap, if one were in tune with events.*
—Robyn Davidson

Living in process is living *our* process and being one
with the process of the universe. Our addictive disease removes us from our connection with the living
process. Our disease alienates us from our spirituality
and our faith and tells us we aren't safe, we have to
control, and we must try to assure security by making
ourselves, our lives, and even the universe static.

We put so much effort into trying to make our universe static that we have not developed the capacity to
be in tune with events. As we learn to tune in and participate, we find that living our process is so much
easier than trying to make the universe static.

———————

WHEN *I am in touch with my process, I am in touch
with the process of the universe.*

FEELING CRAZY

Feeling crazy may be a mark of sanity in my situation.
— Anne Wilson Schaef

Several years ago, after I had written and published *Women's Reality,* I visited an old friend in New York City. After talking a while, she said, "You've changed." (She's an analyst and she always notices things!) "Really," I said, "how?" (I secretly hoped that I had changed. After all, we had not seen each other for several years, and if I hadn't changed, I was in deep trouble!) "You are no longer afraid of being crazy," she observed. "Was I afraid I was crazy?" I asked, somewhat startled. "Yes," she said quietly. "Well, after writing *Women's Reality,* I realize that I have constantly been told that I am crazy by my society when I put forth my clearest, sanest, most precious perceptions. Now I accept that I am 'crazy' in the eyes of an addictive society, and I feel very 'sane' with my 'craziness.'"

WATCH OUT *for who is defining "crazy."*

LETTING GO/RESENTMENTS

Wanna fly, you got to give up the shit that weighs you down.

—Toni Morrison

Our old "shit" is so precious to us. We tenderly harbor our old resentments and periodically throw them pieces of fresh flesh to keep them alive. We nurture our anger. We don't do anything to work it through or let it go, we just hang on and nurture it. And we wonder why we feel so stuck and held back in our lives.

When we hold onto old shit, it weighs us down. It is as if our feet are stuck in fresh tar.

There comes a time when we can see that it doesn't really matter what someone has done to us, our holding onto it is hurting *us* not them, and if we want to heal, we had best take our old shit and fertilize the flowers.

———————————

THE ONLY WAY *to grow is to let go.*

March 4

FEELINGS/FREEDOM

The white fathers told us, "I think therefore I am," and the Black mother within each of us—the poet—whispers in our dreams, I feel, therefore I can be free.
—Audre Lorde

We have been trained to shut off and freeze our feelings. We have been told that feelings are weak and irrational and if we want to be a success in this world, we must be able to control our feelings. The models for success are persons who never have any visible feelings.

Yet when we do this, we find that we are making ourselves more vulnerable, not less. When we push feelings down, we never know when or how they will erupt, and we can rest assured that it will be with greater intensity than if we had acknowledged the original "feeling moment."

Also, feelings are our natural, built-in alarm and information system. It is our feelings not our minds that warn us of danger, that tell us that someone is lying to us, and that tell us of subtle nuances that allow us to discern differences and make decisions. Without this internal information system we can never truly be free.

CELEBRATING *my ability to feel is a way to be fully free.*

LONELINESS

Loneliness and the feeling of being unwanted is the most terrible poverty.

—Mother Teresa

The feeling of loneliness is not uncommon to women who do too much. We are constantly busy and surrounded by people and still we feel lonely. In fact, it is quite possible that one of the reasons that we keep so busy is that we are trying to avoid our feelings of loneliness and are, simultaneously, frightened by intimacy.

We believe if we just rush around enough, keep busy enough, and surround ourselves with enough important and interesting people, our loneliness will disappear. Unfortunately, none of these things works. Indeed, as Fiona Macleod says, "My heart is a lonely hunter that hunts on a lonely hill." Our hearts are seeking something, and the many things we have tried don't seem to be it. When we have lost the connection with our spiritual beings, we will be lonely no matter how much we have.

LONELINESS *is not outside, it's inside.*

RELATIONSHIP

*It has been wisely said that we cannot really love any-
body at whom we never laugh.*

—Agnes Repplier

How serious we are about everything—especially relationships! Often in our most intimate possibilities,
we forget that our laughter at ourselves and at each
other is one of the vehicles that our creator has given
us for grounding ourselves in reality. And relationships that are not grounded in reality don't last.

We have to know others very well to be able to see
their funny sides and to share in the frivolity of family
functions. Let's face it, we human beings are a funny
lot. No robot has ever been capable of the antics we
can think up.

SHARING *my laughter at myself and others is one of
the ways threads of intimacy are spun.*

March 7

SANITY

If, as someone has said, ". . . to be truly civilized, is to embrace disease . . ."

—Robyn Davidson

One of the by-products of living and working in crazy situations is that our tolerance for insanity increases exponentially. Our ability to discern what makes sense and what doesn't becomes impaired. When those around us continually exhibit bizarre behavior, we begin to question our sanity. Often we are not insane. The situation is insane, and we become progressively crazy as we try to adjust to it.

If "to be truly civilized, is to embrace disease," maybe we need to take a look at what we have defined as "civilized."

———————

I AM NOT CRAZY—*it's just that my situation seems to require a crazy person.*

SELF-AFFIRMATION

i found God in myself/& i loved her/i loved her fiercely.
—Ntozake Shange

What better place to find God than within ourselves! It is only when we really know ourselves and affirm ourselves for who we are that we become aware of the divinity that we share with all things. We are part of the hologram . . . we *are* the hologram. When we estrange ourselves from ourselves, we also then lose contact with that which is beyond ourselves.

To know "God" and to love her fiercely is to love ourselves. Loving this God is not loving the self-centered "God" of addiction. It is loving the God that is one, that is within us, and beyond us. It is loving God as we understand God.

CONTACT *with God is so simple, and we make it so difficult.*

SELF-ESTEEM/HIGHER POWER

*Part of my satisfaction and exultation at each erup-
tion was unmistakably feminist solidarity. You men
think you're the only ones that can make a really nasty
mess? You think you got all the firepower and God's on
your side? You think you run things? Watch this, gents.
Watch the Lady act like a woman.*

—Ursula K. Le Guin

In some surprising way, Mount Saint Helens proved
to be an important symbol for all of us. She reminded
us of powers that are unseen and uncontrolled. She
reminded us that there are forces on this planet and in
this universe over which we have no control. We not
only had no control over her eruptions, we could not
even predict what she was going to do next, even
though we applied our best scientific technology and
kept her under constant surveillance. She demonstrated
to our technocratic society that nature (often identi-
fied as female, especially when she's "bad") could not
be controlled.

Although none of us wants destruction to occur or
lives to be lost, we do need occasionally to be reminded
that we are not in charge.

———————————

WHEN SHE SIMMERS *silently, she is like a woman.
When she blows her top off, she is like a woman. We
have a range of responses.*

SERENITY

I am suddenly filled with that sense of peace and meaning which is, I suppose, what the pious have in mind when they talk about the practice of the presence of God.

——Valerie Taylor

When we are operating out of the addictive process, we know little of serenity. The word *serenity* is something that we understand in abstract and often not in practice. As we begin to take care of ourselves and recover from our compulsive doing, we begin to experience *moments* of serenity. The first time we experience serenity, it may zip through our consciousness like a meteor and scare us to death, because this feeling of serenity is so foreign to us. After a while, we begin to recognize these moments of serenity as very special, and we try to *make* them happen through rituals, practices, and techniques. We are now not focusing on controlling the world, we are trying to control our experience of serenity . . . back to the drawing board.

———————————

SERENITY *is a gift. It is available to all of us. It is being one with the presence of God.*

Straightening
the House/Regret

*My tidiness and my untidiness, are full of regret and
remorse and complex feelings.*
                                        —Natalia Ginzburg

One of the greatest gifts that my mother gave me was
that she was a *terrible* housekeeper. She wasn't terrible
at everything, she just was terrible at keeping the
house clean, which she firmly believed that she should
be able to do.

She was a published poet, a great writer of short stories, a painter, a talented breaker and trainer of horses,
an avid reader, a knowledgeable collector of antiques, a
seeker into the psychic and the mysteries of the world,
a good mother, a true, loyal, and devoted friend, incurably curious, an authority on American Indian lore, an
intuitive searcher for precious rocks, fossils, and old
gems, a defender of everyone's civil rights, and most
of all a fascinating and extraordinary woman, but she
couldn't keep the kitchen floor clean.

I was not at all damaged by the state of our house. I
was saddened that she sometimes negatively judged
who she was.

IF NOTHING ELSE, *I hope I can remember what is
important in this life.*

ACCEPTANCE/MISTAKES/AMENDS

Of all the idiots I have met in my life, and the Lord knows that they have not been few or little, I think that I have been the biggest.

—Isak Dinesen

One of the ways that I can reclaim my power and my person is to admit my mistakes. Sometimes it is helpful to sit down and make a list of people that I have wronged (including myself) and to make amends to those with whom it is possible and where it would not harm them to do so.

What a clean feeling it is to accept and own my life and not beat myself up for the mistakes I have made! How good it feels to let those I have harmed know that I am aware of what I have done and that I genuinely wish to own and change my behavior, and do what I can to live clearer and cleaner in the future.

ADMITTING *our mistakes and making amends are powerful tools for reclaiming ourselves.*

SPIRITUAL LIFE

We are not human beings trying to be spiritual. We are spiritual beings trying to be human.

—Jacquelyn Small

So often we try to compartmentalize our spirituality and therefore (hopefully) keep it under control. Our spirituality is much more all-encompassing than many of us care to admit. Everything we do flows from ourselves as spiritual beings. When we make decisions, our spirituality is there. When we interact at work, our spirituality is there. When we wash the dishes, our spirituality is there. So often we have tried to remove our spiritual selves from our daily selves because we equated spirituality with saintliness, and we did not always want saintliness interfering with our daily lives. It is only when we recognize that all that we do is spiritual, that we can let our spirituality inform our humanity.

NOTHING I DO *is too tiny or too tedious to be spiritual.*

ANGER

Fury gathered until I was swollen with it.
                                    —Vera Randal

How many of us know that fury that rises like a ther-
mometer within us until our vocal cords quiver and
our eyes turn a bright red and then glaze over? Young
children and animals always know to scatter at times
like these.

Some of us roll up the windows and scream in our
cars on the highways. Some of us wait until no one is
around and scream into our pillows. Some of us just
scream. Most of us have thought we were crazy at these
times. We're not. We are just alive and responding to
our stressful lives.

A GOOD scream-a-logue not directed at anyone is
often much more effective than a dialogue.

ALONE TIME

When we, as individuals, first rediscover our spirit, we are usually drawn to nurture and cultivate this awareness.

—Shakti Gawain

Alone time is absolutely essential to the human organism. Many of us have been afraid to be alone. We are afraid that if someone else is not around, no one will be present. When we have lost the awareness of ourselves, we try to fill up our time with work, busyness, food, and other people. We have been afraid to sound our own depths. We have been afraid that we would look inside and find no one there.

Yet, when we have that first awareness of "rediscovering our spirit," we know that there is someone there, inside of us, who is well worth knowing.

There is no way to know ourselves unless we have time alone to explore. We need to nurture and protect our alone time even when it seems difficult.

MY ALONE TIME *is as essential to my spirit as food, sleep, and exercise are to my body. I hope I am able to remember that.*

TEARS

I have been told that crying makes me seem soft and therefore of little consequence. As if our softness has to be the price we pay out for power, rather than simply the one that's paid most easily and most often.
—Audre Lorde

Our tears and our softness are not valued much in this society, especially in the work place. In the past, women have been led to believe that we could gain indirect, manipulative power through our tears and our gentle willingness to take care of others.

Many modern women have rejected using our tears and our gentleness to get what we want. Unfortunately, this rejection of our gentler side has resulted in our trying to appear tough and aggressive and in our losing our wholeness.

We are neither all soft nor all tough. We just are.

———————————

SHARING *my tears and softness is an act of love. Sharing my strength and assertiveness is also an act of love. When I share me, I am loving.*

BECOMING/ACCEPTANCE

*The great thing about getting older is that you don't
lose all the other ages you've been.*
            —Madeline L'Engle

Life is a process. We are a process. Everything that has
happened in our lives has happened for a reason and is
an integral part of our becoming.

One of the challenges of our lives is to integrate
the pieces of our lives as we live them. It is sometimes
tempting to try to deny huge periods of our lives or
forget significant events, especially if they have been
painful. To try to erase our past is to rob ourselves of
our own hard-earned wisdom.

There is not a child or an adolescent within us.
There is the child or adolescent who has grown into us.

When we realize that among the most important
strengths that we bring to our work are the life experiences we have had and the ages we have been, maybe
we will not resent getting older.

MY WISDOM EMERGES *as I accept and integrate all
that I have been and all that has happened to me.*

AWARENESS

For me, it's a constant discipline to remember to go back inside to connect with my intuition.
                                                    —Shakti Gawain

Each of us has much more brainpower than we ever use. We have so overdeveloped the logical/rational/linear parts of our brains that we frequently have left undeveloped our awareness, intuition, and creativity. We sometimes even forget that awareness, intuition, and creativity *are* brain functions.

Yet, even without being valued and exercised, these aspects of our selves remain faithful and do not leave us. Whenever we open ourselves to our intuition, it is always there. It is important that we remember to go back inside to connect with our intuition. Trusting our intuition often saves us from disaster.

IT IS SOMETIMES *frightening to trust my intuition. It is always disastrous* not *to trust it.*

UNREALISTIC PROMISES/DESPAIR

We workaholics make so many promises that no human being could possibly keep them. That is one of the ways we keep ourselves feeling bad about ourselves.

—Lynn

One of the problems that we workaholics and careaholics have is that we overextend ourselves and believe that we can and should be able to fulfill the promises we make. We want to be nice. We want to be members of the team. We want to be seen as competent and dependable.

We also hate to say no when someone notices us and has the confidence in us to ask us to do something. We *want* to be able to deliver.

Yet, when we do not check out with ourselves whether we can or want to fulfill our promises, we end up overcommitting ourselves and ultimately feeling bad about ourselves, which just feeds our self-esteem problems.

————————

CHECKING *to see if I can and want to fulfill a promise before I make it is good for me and good for others.*

FEELINGS/CONTROL

For years I have endeavored to calm an impetuous tide—laboring to make my feelings take an orderly course—it was striving against the stream.
> —Mary Wollstonecraft

We have generally been taught that feelings are bad. They aren't logical and rational. They are unruly, messy, unpredictable, and often intense. How wonderful to have such a range of expression!

Often, as children, it was not just our feelings of anger, rage, sadness, or pouting that were stifled. We were told to be quiet and equally commanded to suppress our feelings of excitement, joy, creativity, imagination, giggles, laughter, and happiness. Strangely enough, we have found that it is not possible to suppress some feelings and not others. When we push down anger, joy goes with it. When we push down rage, tenderness goes with it.

We are often told as adults that our anger must be appropriate, nonoffensive, justified, and expressed in the right way. What a joke. Trying to girdle my feelings is like trying to tie down the wind.

WHEN I *ignore and suppress my feelings, they come out in frightening, sometimes destructive ways. I need to learn to honor them . . . whatever they are.*

FORGIVENESS

If you haven't forgiven yourself something, how can you forgive others?

—Dolores Huerta

Forgiveness has to start with the self. To forgive ourself does not mean that we condone or support everything we have done. It means that we own it. We claim it. We accept that we were in the wrong, and we move on.

Often, when we recognize that we are in the wrong, we slip into our self-centeredness, becoming so absorbed and arrogant in berating ourselves that we never quite reach a stage of forgiveness. To forgive we have to let go and move on. If we do not know how to do that with ourselves, we can never forgive others.

———————

*"*TO ERR *is human, to forgive divine." To forgive myself and others is divinely human.*

PATIENCE/DECISIONS

Our most important decisions are discovered, not made.
We can make the unimportant ones but the major ones
require us to wait with the discovery.
                                    —Anne Wilson Schaef

We often push ourselves to decisions that have not
ripened and are not ready to be made. We castigate
ourselves for being indecisive, and others share this
opinion of us. We believe that if we were just wise
enough, intelligent enough, or clear enough we would
know what we want. We do not respect that maybe
the reason we can't make a decision is because we *don't
know yet.*

For many generations, women have felt that we had
to say yes to everything. Then we learned that it is OK
to say no, so we have practiced saying no. Unfortunately, however, it is still exceedingly difficult for us
to say "I don't know" and to feel comfortable staying
with our not knowing, until we do know.

THE QUALITY *of my decisions is directly proportionate to my patience with my not knowing.*

HANGING IN THERE

To be somebody you must last.
                                            —Ruth Gordon

We women who do too much know how to "hang in there." We stick with a situation that a sane person would have given up on years ago. This persistence is, indeed, often a part of our insanity. We get so fixated on hanging in that we lose perspective and fail to see that our very persistence may be exacerbating a sick situation. If we withdraw from the situation, organizations in which we are involved might have the opportunity to test their reality, or they may even be allowed to "hit bottom" and come out the other side.

We accept the virtue of perseverance but unfortunately our dedication to it has affected our judgment and our ability to discern what is really needed.

———————————

IN SOME *situations it is better to leave; in some it is important to persevere, in some we simply have to wait and see. The trick is to discern which is which.*

GRATITUDE

You love like a coward. Don't take no steps at all. Just stand around and hope for things to happen outright. Unthankful and unknowing like a hog under an acorn tree. Eating and grunting with your ears hanging over your eyes, and never even looking up to see where the acorns are coming from.

—Zora Neale Hurston

So often we go through life like hogs. We root around and munch on the goodies around us without ever once acknowledging where they come from or that we are receiving them as gifts.

The process of the universe is so generous with us that we take too much for granted. We "love like cowards." We expect everyone and everything around us to take risks, while we *take*. We become so arrogant that we convince ourselves that everything that we have is a gift from us to us. We don't stop to see that we couldn't be munching those tasty acorns unless there were some celestial oak tree dropping them.

———

TODAY, *I have the opportunity to stop, look up, and be grateful for the many gifts that are mine.*

BUSYNESS

*My husband and I have figured out a really good sys-
tem about the housework: neither one of us does it.*
—Dottie Archibald

I wonder if this would work. Have I ever had the courage and security to let my housework go for several
years, to see if there was a natural limit to the amount
of dirt that accumulated? Nope, and I'm not sure I
want to.

Yet, how much of the constant repetitive housework I do is because of my need to keep busy and not
because it actually needs to be done?

One of the characteristics of a workaholic is procrastination. Often, our busyness is a subtle form of
procrastination that keeps us away from what we *really* need to be doing.

I AM GRATEFUL *for the things I hear which give me
the opportunity to shift my perception ever so slightly.*

COURAGE/FEAR

Courage—fear that has said its prayers.
                                        —Dorothy Bernard

I wonder if it is possible to be in touch with our true courageousness without being in touch with our spirituality? We know how to be foolhardy. We know how to take risks. We even know how to put ourselves on the line.

But do we know how to soar through the tempering fires of our fear, reach deep into our spirit, and find the courage that is there? Do we have the courage for the dailiness of life? Can we admit a mistake and not give in to the luxury of self-castigation? Do we have the courage to be honest about who we really are with those we love? Do we have the courage to return a bad piece of meat to the butcher, or do we just grumble?

When we face our fears and let ourselves know our connection to the power that is in us and beyond us, we learn courage.

———————————

MY COURAGE *is everyday just like my spirituality.*

DISCOURAGEMENT

Only the dusty flowers, the clank of censers and tracks,
leading from somewhere to nowhere.
>   —Anna Akhmatova

What a beautiful expression of discouragement! . . .
Tracks that lead from somewhere to nowhere. We have
all tried so hard to do the right things. We have gone
to the right schools, followed the rules, worked long
hours, skipped long showers . . . and for what? . . .
tracks that lead from somewhere (with dusty flowers
along the way), or perhaps even tracks that lead from
nowhere to nowhere.

Relax. Of course we feel discouraged at times. Recovery is more like a spiral than a line. Our struggles
offer us the opportunity to become better acquainted
with the many facets of our disease.

———————————

RECOVERY *doesn't have to be a straight line. As long*
as I am on the road, I must be going somewhere.

DESPAIR
STEP THREE

If God is a fly on the wall, Nanny, hand me a fly swatter.

—Gaby Brimmer

Even Jesus felt forsaken by God. We can identify with him. We have been angry with God, and we have abandoned our Higher Power because we felt abandoned. This God on whom we want to depend simply refuses to live our lives for us. We want to turn it all over to our Higher Power and lie back and relax, and old H.P. is not cooperating.

Where's the fly swatter? If my Higher Power won't do it my way, to hell with it.

Right! Enjoying ourselves, are we? Isn't this fun? A fight with God—that should keep us occupied for quite some time.

———————————

WHEN I FEEL *abandoned by my Higher Power, I am the one who has gone away.*

PASSION

It is the soul's duty to be loyal to its own desires. It must abandon itself to its master passion.

—Rebecca West

Many competent women have a difficult time distinguishing between passion and workaholism. When we hear the emerging concern about the lethal effects of compulsive working, we almost always ask ourselves (or justify to ourselves): "But what about being passionate about my work? Are you saying that to be passionate about my work is to be a workaholic? I don't want to give up my work."

Many of our role models for success are people who were willing to be devoured by their work. This is confusing to us.

True passion and doing what is important for us to do does not require us to destroy ourselves in the process. In fact, it is when passion gets distorted to compulsivity that it is destructive.

———————————

MY PASSION *feeds me. My addictiveness devours me. There is a great difference between the two.*

BECOMING

A clay pot sitting in the sun will always be a clay pot. It has to go through the white heat of the furnace to become porcelain.

———Mildred Witte Stouven

Actually, there's nothing wrong with being a clay pot. It's just that all of us have the possibility of becoming porcelain. And it isn't quite so simple as just being fired or not being fired. Some of us explode in the kiln. Some of us collapse before we ever reach the kiln, and some of us develop horrible cracks that seriously threaten our utilitarian value.

Yet probably the saddest response is to have gone through the firing and to refuse to become porcelain. All of us have furnaces in our lives. Not all of us glean the lessons from the firing.

———————

IT IS *our faith that facilitates our surrender to the firing.*

Pain/Suffering

Flowers grow out of dark moments.
—Corita Kent

Pain is inevitable in life. As we begin to recover, we can see that much of the suffering that we experience is directly related to our stubbornness and illusion of control. The more we hold on to issues, beliefs, or experiences that we long since have grown beyond, the harder we have to get "whacked along side the head" to get the learning. Contrary to much religious belief, suffering is not noble. It is often just plain stupid and comes out of our stubbornness and need to control.

When we are attached to our suffering, we often miss those "flowers that grow out of dark moments."

———————

MY SUFFERING *teaches me about my disease. My pain teaches me about my life.*

April 1

GIFTS

April
Comes like an idiot, babbling, and strewing flowers.
　　　　　—Edna St. Vincent Millay

One of the gifts of life is the changing of the weather and the seasons. As we relinquish some of our illusions of control, we realize that each change of the weather and each season of the year have many gifts in store for us, if we participate in them and live with them. When we fight and struggle against the weather and the seasons, we dissipate the energy that could be used for enjoyment.

April does seem to enter "like an idiot" sometimes . . . a playful, energetic, sparkling idiot that brings in riots . . . riots of flowers. Summer gives us longer days to enjoy and a time for laziness, if we accept the offers of summer. Fall gathers in, and winter cozies in. In living with the seasons, we receive many gifts.

———————————

ACCEPTING *nature's gift of the seasons is like opening brightly colored packages loosely tied with crinkled ribbons.*

April 2

LIVING LIFE FULLY

Don't be afraid your life will end: be afraid that it will never begin.

—Grace Hansen

So often our focus upon death and the possibility of dying is an escape from our real fear . . . that of living our lives.

We have become comfortable with a way of life that is actually a slow death. Our constant working, busyness, taking care of others, and rushing around relieves us of the responsibility of being fully alive and kills us slowly, and in a socially acceptable way to boot. What more could we ask from an addiction?

Why are we so afraid of living our lives? What would our lives be like if we decided to show up for them and live them? Why is it so frightening to anticipate feeling our feelings and being present to each moment?

MY INNER PROCESS *never gives me more than I can handle. I may not like handling it, and I can handle it. It is when I refuse to handle my life that it backs up on me.*

CONFUSED THINKING: STEP TWO

Any addiction is a falling into unconsciousness.
                              —Marion Woodman

Some of us want to deny what happens to our thinking processes as we become progressively addicted. It is easy for us to see how alcohol and drugs affect our thinking. We are even open to the possibility that nicotine, caffeine, and sugar affect the way we think. But overworking, rushing around, compulsively taking care of others, can these *activities* really affect the way we think? *Yes, they can and do!*

In Twelve-Step circles we often hear the words "stinkin' thinkin'" used to describe the thinking processes of the addict. We lose our ability to make judgments, we become "unconscious," we obsess, and we become "insane." We do the same thing again and again, even when it has always failed. This is *insanity*. Any, I repeat, any addiction can result in insanity, unconsciousness, and lack of judgment.

HOW *can I make myself better if I am confused, unconscious, and insane?* I can't. *That is why I may be ready to see the need for a power greater than myself that can restore me to sanity.*

INTEGRITY/SUCCESS: STEP FOUR

Integrity is so perishable in the summer months of success.

—Vanessa Redgrave

I wonder, have I let my integrity slip in order to succeed? Have there been times when I was willing to look the other way or take the easy way out in order to avoid conflict or to gain acceptance?

Every day we are offered opportunities to sacrifice our integrity on issues that may be of the utmost importance or on ones that appear insignificant. Without our integrity, there is no way that we can feel good about ourselves. Success and loss of integrity are not synonymous. In fact, true success requires great integrity.

These "little" incidents of integrity slippage eat away at us like termites. How important it is to stop and take a look at the decisions we have made! What a relief it is to know that our valued integrity is there deep within us and that we can reconnect with it at a moment's notice.

CHECKING *for possible slips of integrity allows me to feel better about myself.*

April 5

CONNECTEDNESS

The motions and patterns and connections of things became apparent on a gut level.
—Robyn Davidson

Each of us has magical moments in our lives when we become aware of the oneness of all things. When that happens, we see the "motions and patterns and connections." A feeling of warmth permeates our being and we heave a sigh of heartfelt relief. We can know the unknowable. We *know* the unknowable.

Yet when we try to share these experiences, we find ourselves inarticulate. In our feeble attempts to describe them, words seem like balls of cotton growing larger and larger as we try to push them out of our mouths. Often, in talking about such an experience, we lose our connection with the experience itself.

———————

I WILL TRUST *these profound pauses. And I know that I cannot have them unless I pause.*

FAILURE

The clouds gathered together, stood still and watched the river scuttle around the forest floor, crash head-long into haunches of hills with no notion of where it was going, until exhausted, ill and grieving, it slowed to a stop just twenty leagues short of the sea.
—Toni Morrison

My, can that woman write! I read a passage like the one above, and I just want to read it over and over. It is such a beautiful description of how we sometimes bash and batter ourselves in trying to reach a goal and then end up "ill and grieving" and exhausted, not real-izing that we are almost there. We, like the river, rush helter-skelter, headlong into the barriers of our being.

———————————

NONE OF US *can avoid* failure. We can *avoid bat-tering ourselves in the process.*

April 7

MONOTONE MINDS

Life ought to be a struggle of desire toward adventures whose nobility will fertilize the soul.
—Rebecca West

One of the side effects of doing too much is developing monotone minds. We spend so much time in our work and in work-related activities that our awarenesses and our perceptions become narrower and narrower. We reach a point where we can't talk about anything but our work and, if the truth be known, we don't *want* to talk about anything but our work.

We have become dull and uninteresting. We may even find that we're bored with ourselves. This happens to those of us who work full time at home, and it happens to those who sit at the top of a corporation.

We have taken a rainbow and compressed it into a solid, uninteresting beam of light.

———————————

THE TEARS *for myself may be the prism needed to rediscover the rainbow that is me.*

April 8

FRIENDSHIP

*She became for me an island of light, fun, wisdom
where I could run with my discoveries and torments
and hopes at any time of day and find welcome.*
                                        —May Sarton

We sometimes forget all the friends we have had in
our lives. The negative thinking of our disease tends
to focus on what is missing. But let's take today and let
ourselves remember the friends who have been there
for us.

For me, there was the little old lady with the beautiful flower garden who would not let my parents
spank me when I tried to pick some flowers and inad-
vertently pulled them up by the roots. "She was only
admiring their beauty," she said when my mother
marched me over to apologize. And there was the
friend in grade school who came forward to share
the rap when I was the only one caught. There were
friends who shared our tentative relationships and sexual explorations and never told. There were friends we
studied with, hung out with, and grew up with—who
were there for us. There were adults who served as
models and mentors and judged us not. There were
friends.

REMEMBERING *the friends I have had in my life
caresses my mind and being like a warm bath caresses
my body.*

BELIEF/GREATER POWER
STEP TWO

*The prayer that reforms the sinner and heals the sick is
an absolute faith that all things are possible to God.*
　　　　　　　　　　　　　—Mary Baker Eddy

Step Two of the Twelve-Step program states that we
"came to believe that a power greater than ourselves
could restore us to sanity." That's a tough one.

As we have climbed the ladder of success, we have
discovered that one of the subtle requirements is the
development of a certain sophisticated, scientific cyn-
icism. We no longer want to appear or be innocent,
and we believe that the only other choice is to become cynical and "scientific." Thank goodness we have
the option of leaving both our innocent gullibility and
our cynical sophistication behind. We can let ourselves believe that all things are possible . . . not con-
trollable—possible.

———————————

PART *of my "insanity" is not seeing that my life has
become insane and not believing that I can return to
sanity.*

April 10

DUTY

Ah, duty is an icy shadow.

—Augusta Evans

Many are the crimes that have been committed in the name of duty. Ministers neglect their children in the name of duty. People kill one another in the name of duty. We abandon ourselves and our dreams in the name of duty. We feed our addiction by overworking and then justify our behavior as our duty to our family. We batter our bodies in the name of duty. Duty becomes the excuse for much of our addictive life.

We addicts will use anything for a fix. We will take the most noble idea and turn it into a nightmare to perpetuate our addictions. We are tricky, and the disease is tricky.

When we use duty to batter ourselves and others, it has, indeed, become an "icy shadow."

I DON'T WANT *to be loved out of duty. Do you?*

BUSYNESS/RUSHING/DISTRACTIBILITY
STEP ONE

*A mark of a true workaholic is cleaning house in your
underwear.*

—Coleen

We workaholics can see so many unfinished projects
and so many things that need to be done that we are
easily distracted. Getting dressed in the morning is
not always an easy process. We take our shower, and
then we see something that needs to be done. We get
our underwear on, and then we see something that
needs to be done. It is difficult to focus on the task at
hand, and when we do, we see a million other little
things that we'll just tidy up before we get dressed.

Surely we have time to pick up the papers on the
way to the kitchen to get our morning coffee. On the
way back to the bathroom we can straighten the pillows on the couch. If we put the laundry in now, it can
run while we do a quick vacuum.

Is it any wonder that we secretly see ourselves as
incompetent? Even though we get a lot of little tasks
done, we are so distractible that we jump from one
task to another and never have a real feeling of completion. It is helpful to remember that our disease is
busyness and distractibility. It is only in recognizing
these behaviors as part of a disease and not truly who
we are that we open ourselves to the possibility of recovery.

I AM POWERLESS *over these behaviors and my admission of my powerlessness is the first step toward health.*

WEEKENDS/UNSTRUCTURED TIME

*I hate weekends. There's no structure. There's no com-
pass. How will I know what to do if I don't have to
do it?*

—Susan

Weekends are awful for women who do too much.
We miss the structure of the work week. We do not
like the lack of schedule, and we feel lost without our
work.

To avoid experiencing these feelings, we have developed certain insurance strategies. We bring work
home. We schedule our weekend projects and activities so that we almost have the secure feeling of being
at work. We panic and go into the office to "pick up
some things and tie up some loose ends."

WHAT *are we afraid of? . . . ourselves?*

ADRENALINE/BUSYNESS

They sicken of the calm that know the storm.
—Dorothy Parker

Ah, that adrenaline rush! How we love it! We are so accustomed to dealing with crisis that we get nervous when things get calm.

Many women who are recovering from workaholism and doing too much are beginning to recognize that they have become addicted to their own adrenaline rush. We used to get a "buzz" with the excitement of a new project or an impending deadline. We functioned best under pressure (or so we believed). We got nervous and tense when our lives became too quiet. We needed the emotional arousal. We needed our fix.

Fortunately, we began to see that our adrenaline rushes were exhausting our bodies and our beings. Our addiction to our own adrenaline was as destructive to our bodies as drugs or alcohol. Recovery from adrenaline addiction has been a slow, painful process. Yet, we have the hope of a new life and the possibility of living it in a healthy body.

———————

I HAVE DISCOVERED *that what I used to call numbness may just be contentment, and contentment feels great.*

TAKING STOCK/GRATITUDE
STEP FOUR

Long-term change requires looking honestly at our lives and realizing that it's nice to be needed, but not at the expense of our health, our happiness, and our sanity.

—Ellen Sue Stern

There is no quick fix to any addiction, and workaholism, rushaholism, busyaholism, and careaholism *are* addictions. Part of the "stinkin' thinkin'" of the addict is to want a quick fix. *There is none.* Even wanting the quick fix is part of the disease.

The twelve steps work, and it is possible for us to live serene, happy, and productive lives. But recovery takes time. There are many hills and valleys along the way, and if we keep going to meetings, calling our sponsor, and working the program, we find that we do have a connection with a power greater than ourselves, and our lives get better.

———————

I AM SO *fortunate to have the support of a program that works and the company of others to travel this journey with me.*

ACCEPTANCE/HONESTY

With him for a sire and her for a dam,
What should I be but just what I am?
                    —Edna St. Vincent Millay

Some of us do not know the difference between putting ourselves down, thus refusing to accept our gifts and talents, and accepting who we are.

Indeed, we often bounce between being worthless and being totally arrogant. Interestingly, feeling "like a piece of shit" and feeling that we are unique and wonderful are intimately related. In both illusions, we refuse to see ourselves as we really are.

It is only when we are able to say, "I know nothing about that," or "I am really good at doing that and quite knowledgeable about that," that we are moving toward acceptance of self. Seeing our shortcomings allows us to accept them. Accepting our strengths allows us to soar. Honesty about self is the key.

———————

TODAY *I have the opportunity not to be grandiose about either my shortcomings or my capabilities. I can be me.*

April 16

INDEPENDENCE

Dependency invites encroachment.
—Patricia Meyer Spacks

We women who do too much are terrified of being dependent. We clearly understand that "dependency invites encroachment." Unfortunately, our fear of dependency often results in behavior that looks like independence but is really what the psychologists call counterdependence. We are so afraid of dependency that we can't trust anyone, which means that we are still controlled by our dependency needs. Whenever we are circling around any form of dependency, whether it be dependence, independence, or interdependence, we probably are in trouble.

Another option is not to define ourselves in terms of dependency. We can learn to be self-defining. We can learn not to ask others to form our identities for us. Only then can we be truly free and bring the gift of ourselves to any relationship.

INDEPENDENCE *and dependence may both be cages.*

HEALING

The new space . . . has a kind of invisibility to those who have not entered it.

—Mary Daly

It is especially difficult for women who do too much to consider willingly entering the unknown. Like any addict, we like to keep everything under control, and we certainly don't want even to start a journey without an accurate road map. Unfortunately, recovery doesn't work that way. Recovery is a leap of faith.

Most of us, because we grew up in dysfunctional families, work in addictive settings, and live in an addictive society, don't have experiential knowledge of what it's like to live our process, live sobriety, or live out of our clarity. Yet many people are making that leap of faith and taking the first step on the road to recovery. We know that there has to be something better. We have a vague recollection of something. We can't quite remember what it is, and we know it is there. One of the true present-day miracles is that so many are beginning recovery when we really have no clear idea of what recovery is.

I HAVE WISHED *for a miracle, and I can be one.*

APPRECIATION

*And to all those voices of wisdom that have whispered
to me along the way.*

—Dhyani Ywahoo

Gratitude and appreciation are important facets of our
lives. There have been so many women who have
shared their wisdom and their knowledge with us.
Some of that wisdom has been learned from others,
and some of it has been self-taught, and all of it has
been profound.

Remember the neighbor who taught us how to
care for plants? Remember the mother who shared
some helpful hints about staying out of the way of our
children? Remember that little old lady in our place
of worship who quietly seemed to live what we were
being taught about spirituality? Remember that book
that seemed just to appear when we needed it? There
have been voices of wisdom all around us all our lives.

PERHAPS, *as one of my wise friends says, "It's time to
have a gratitude attack."*

RUSHING AND HURRYING

Sometimes I wish I had suction cups to hold me down.
—Pam

Sometimes we really do feel powerless over our need to rush around and keep busy, and we just wish there were some way to stop ourselves. Our life truly feels overwhelming and unmanageable.

We are amazed at how relieved we feel when we can actually admit that we are powerless over this crazy behavior and our lives just are not working the way we would like them to work.

We are powerful women, *and* we are powerless over our crazy lives.

What a consolation it is to know that a power greater than ourselves *can* restore us to sanity. What a relief it is to know that our admission that our lives are insane right now opens the door to sanity.

What a relief it is to sigh and know that, as we turn our lives and wills over to that power greater than ourselves, we have the path to renewed sanity before us.

SUCTION CUPS *probably won't help much anyway, but turning our lives over sounds like an option with real possibilities.*

April 20

REALITY/INVENTORY

You need to claim the events of your life to make yourself yours. When you truly possess all you have been and done, which may take some time, you are fierce with reality.

—Flonda Scott Maxwell

Being "fierce with reality" requires that we break through our denial about ourselves and our lives layer by layer. At some point in our lives, we need to stop and take a thorough inventory of who we are and what we have done. This fearless and searching inventory not only focuses upon the things that we have done wrong and the things we wish we had done in some other way, it also focuses upon our strengths and the things we have done right.

So many of us forget that taking stock of ourselves also means writing down what is good about us and the things we appreciate and like about ourselves. After all, honesty is not only about the mistakes, it is also about the good, the powerful, the creative, the loving, and the gentle, compassionate aspects of ourselves.

WHEN WE STOP *and truly possess all we have been, and done, we are on the path to becoming who we are.*

SELF-AWARENESS

Until the missing story of ourselves is told, nothing besides told can suffice us: we shall go on quietly craving it.

—Laura Riding

Probably the most important journey we will ever take is the journey inward. Unless we know who we are, how can we possibly offer what we have?

Each of us is a unique combination of heredity and experiences. No one else has to offer what we have to offer. Yet, if we do not have the self-awareness to undergrid our uniqueness, we never make our contribution.

One of the most disastrous effects of our disease is that we never really have the time for the process of self-awareness, and then, when we do, we may be too exhausted to care.

———————————

I NEED *to know my story . . . all of it.*

SELF-RESPECT

When self-respect takes its rightful place in the psyche of woman, she will not allow herself to be manipulated by anyone.

—Indira Mahindra

Being a woman isn't always the easiest thing in the world, but it's what I have to work with right now. There are so many aspects of ourselves that merit self-respect. We are unbelievably competent at what we do. We are flexible and strong and can be both simultaneously. We have good ideas that are practical and creative, and we can articulate them well. We have the ability to deal with several tasks simultaneously and attend to each one. We are organizers, creators, and doers and we have a great capacity for being. We have much to contribute including a perspective on life that is different from that of the men around us. We are here to stay, and we and others need to accept that fact.

———————

MY SELF-RESPECT *is not only essential to me, it is important to the world.*

GUILT

Shit work is infinitely safe. In exchange for doing it you can extract an unconscionable return . . . the women's pound of flesh.

—Colette Dowling

We are often experts in guilt. Certainly we have learned it from masters. We unquestionably and with great doggedness go about our assigned tasks without a grumble or a reproach.

We are armed, however, with our sighs, our clenched teeth, our pathetic looks of acceptance, and our sagging shoulders. Our favorite phrase is, "That's okay," but we really don't mean it. One of our greatest skills is suffering, and we do it so well. We get our pound of flesh, and we lose our souls in the process.

TELL ME, *is it really worth it? Are we ready to give up the guilt game? It gets infinitely boring.*

BEING PROJECTLESS

Out of the strain of the Doing,
Into the peace of the Done.
> —Julia Louise Woodruff

When most women finish a task, they heave a sigh of relief, pat themselves on the back, and give themselves a well-deserved break. Not so for women who do too much. The "peace of the Done" simply does not compute. There is no experience to which we can relate this concept.

Fortunately, as we let ourselves see that we are not just talking about doing too much, we begin to have a different perspective.

We begin to learn that completion and beginning are not the same process. We begin to see that the completion of an important project has every right to be dignified by a natural grieving process. Something that required the best of us has ended. We will miss it.

BEING PROJECTLESS *and being worthless are not synonymous.*

April 25

BELIEF

*The experience of God, or in any case the possibility of
experiencing God, is innate.*

—Alice Walker

We cry to a God "out there," and our voices return
like burned-out space ships that have traversed the
universe. We ask authorities how to experience God
and realize that they have come to worship their rituals and techniques, yet seem to know little of God.
No ancient prophet lost in the wilderness felt more
isolated than we do as we buzz around the wilderness
of our cities and organizations. How could any God
get through this steel and concrete?

Yet, when we stop, we have a glimmer of understanding of what it means to say that "the possibility of
experiencing God, *is innate.*" We do not have to look
for that possibility. It is already in us.

———————————

THE POSSIBILITY *of experiencing a power greater
than myself has always been there, knocking on my
inner door.*

April 26

BUSYNESS

The season is changeable, fitful, and maddening as I am myself these days that are cloaked with too many demands and engagements.

—May Sarton

When we do not recognize that we have become too busy and overextended, we too find ourselves being "changeable, fitful, and maddening." Our lack of awareness of our needs and our inability to attend to them sets up a situation where our only recourse is to become so obnoxious that others will leave us alone. Then we do not have to take the responsibility for stating that we need time to ourselves and taking it. Of course, this particular technique for getting alone time usually results in fences that need to be mended.

There are other ways of having what we need. We can let ourselves know that we need time to ourselves and then we can arrange to have it.

TAKING THE TIME *I need for myself when I need it may be a lot less exciting than creating a crisis, and it certainly is less messy.*

Choices/Feeling Trapped

I discovered I always have choices and sometimes it's only a choice of attitude.
—Judith M. Knowlton

One of the most devastating characteristics of the addictive process is that our perceptions, our judgment, and our thinking become so distorted that we come to believe that we have no choices and are completely trapped. We have the illusion that there are only two choices (usually to stay or leave) and neither looks attractive.

We do have options. We do have choices, even if the only choice available at the moment is to see that we are stuck and to accept that "stuckness." Amazingly, when we truly accept our stuckness, our situations begin to change. Often it is not the situation that is keeping us stuck but our *attitude* about our situation.

CHOICES *are part of being human. When I feel I have no choices, I am probably operating out of my disease.*

April 28

BEAUTY

Oh, it was a glorious morning! I suppose the best kind
of spring morning is the best weather God has to offer.
It certainly helps one to believe in Him [sic].
                                            —Dodie Smith

How long has it been since we have allowed ourselves
to rejoice in a beautiful day? How long has it been
since we allowed ourselves to notice that it even *is* a
beautiful day?

Those of us who live and work in cities have given
ourselves obstacles that challenge us to have to work a
little harder even to notice what kind of day it is.

For women who do too much, the beautiful day
may be noteworthy only in the absence of hassle that
rain or snow might present. A beautiful day, then, only
becomes the vehicle to get more done. There are other
options.

I LONG *for the awareness to say, "Oh, it was a glori-*
ous morning!"

April 29

FEAR/MANIPULATION

*All women hustle. Women watch faces, voices, gestures,
moods. The person who has to survive through cunning.*
—Marge Piercy

Most women are accomplished research scientists. We
have developed skills for gathering data that would put
most researchers to shame. We are constantly scanning
faces, bodies, and situations for clues about what is acceptable and what we can get away with. We have, unfortunately, in many situations become people who
"survive through cunning." Our hyperalertness em-
anates from our fear that whatever we do will not be
enough—our fear that *we* are not enough no matter
what we do. We have to be cunning to survive, or so
we have come to believe. Some have said that this revolution of women is the only revolution where the
outpost of the enemy is in our own heads.

I AM ENOUGH. *We all will just have to accept what
I have to give.*

April 30

ISOLATION

One of the reasons our society has become such a mess is that we're isolated from each other.
—Maggie Kuhn

Isolation is one of the characteristics of addiction. Isolation is one of the characteristics of women who do too much.

We may be surrounded by people all day long but our singleminded dedication to our work isolates us. We do not like to be interrupted by friends. We would rather get our work done. We get angry when things don't fall into place, and others are afraid to approach us.

We have become just as locked up and closeted with our working, our busyness, our hurrying around as any alcoholic is with her bottle. We have forgotten how to reach out, and we don't have the time for it, even if we remember how. We think if we just had more time to focus on our work we'd feel better, and instead we feel exhausted. Isolation is an energy drain.

I NEED to learn the difference between isolation and solitude.

TODAY

Normal day, let me be aware of the treasure you are. Let me learn from you, love you, bless you before you depart. Let me not pass you by in quest of some rare and perfect tomorrow. Let me hold you while I may, for it may not always be so. One day I shall dig my nails into the earth, or bury my face in the pillow, or stretch myself taut, or raise my hands to the sky and want, more than all the world, your return.

—Mary Jean Iron

This moment is right now. It is what we have. How often we have squandered the treasure of today and dreamed of the fortunes of the future, only to mourn for the loss of this day. Today, we can see the excitement in the eyes of a child over some new discovery. Today, we can listen to an old friend before we get on to the next task. Have we missed today by not being present to it? Will we later weep tears of mourning and wish for its return? How much better to live it today.

———————————

JUST *a normal day—what a gift!*

COURAGE

Remember, Ginger Rogers did everything Fred Astaire did, but she did it backwards and in high heels.
                                            —Faith Whittlesey

That's right! Ginger Rogers was amazingly good at what she did, and so are we. It takes courage for women to acknowledge how good we are at what we do. We are caught in a strange cultural expectation of having to be simultaneously competent and passive. This often results in a kind of humility that really is a denial of our expertise.

Also, women who do too much seem to vacillate between exaggerating our competence and feeling that we are worthless and totally incompetent. This vacillation between extremes is part of the addictive disease.

The real test of courage is being realistic and letting ourselves know that we really are competent at many things.

———————————

BEING GOOD *at what we do isn't a curse. It's a gift that comes from ourselves* and *from a power greater than ourselves.*

DESPAIR

That was a time when only the dead could smile.
                                        —Anna Akhmatova

We have known times like these. In fact, the point
where we realized that we had to admit that doing too
much was no longer something that *we* did, *it did us,*
and was our personal moment of hitting bottom. Before we completely admitted our powerlessness over
our working too much, we despaired, fearing that nothing could change.

Yet we *have* changed. We have reached the depths
of despair and lived through it. We have gone into the
abyss and found that God is nothingness too.

We remember our despair, and we are also grateful
to it because hitting bottom in our disease has paved
the way for our recovery, and recovery is great!

I NEVER THOUGHT *I would be grateful for this
disease, and it has opened up a possibility of a whole
new life for me.*

May 4

LIVING IN THE PRESENT

Yesterday is a cancelled check
Tomorrow is a promissory note
Today is cash in hand; spend it wisely.

—Anonymous

What a challenge to live in the present! We are often so busy killing the present moment with worries about tomorrow or regrets about yesterday that we kill our todays. Ironically, all we can really do is be in the present.

Living in the present means noticing—noticing when we are tired, noticing when we need to go the bathroom, noticing when we need to rest.

Living in the present means taking a walk for the sake of the walk, not just to get someplace. Living in the present means noticing and appreciating our now. Living in the present means doing our lives, not thinking about them.

IF I DO MY LIFE *then I won't be undone.*

May 5

FEELING OVERWHELMED

The social workers have named a new syndrome. It's called "compassion fatigue." Why does it sound so familiar?

—Anne Wilson Schaef

Careaholics never quite know when it all happened. We were trained to believe that, if we just took care of people and listened and understood, they in turn would take care of us. We firmly believed that relationships are built on people taking care of each other, and if we took care first, we would certainly get the same in return. What a shock to find out that this belief is not only not held by everyone, but the more we take care of people, the more they want.

We feel drained, resentful, taken advantage of, and overwhelmed. Those seem to be normal feelings in the situation. Thank goodness we don't have to stay stuck there, however. Just recognizing the feelings helps us begin to check out our assumptions about caretaking.

———————

LOVING *isn't caretaking and caretaking isn't love. We can't buy love . . . it's a gift.*

GRATITUDE

Make a prayer acknowledging yourself as a vehicle of light, giving thanks for the good that has come that day and an affirmation of intent to live in harmony with all your relations.

—Dhyani Ywahoo

As we begin to recover and get clearer, we are often overcome with moments of gratitude. We begin to see the possibility that we are not our disease. We have the disease of overworking and doing too much, and that is not who we are. We begin to see that we do have moments of clarity, and we truly like the person we experience during those moments. We begin to see the good that we do each day and the good that comes to us each day. We have times of deep, heartfelt gratitude and love for ourselves, our family, our friends, and the world around us. We even begin to have a glimmer of what it would mean to live in harmony with all those around us. We are healing.

———————

I CAN TRULY *give thanks for the good that is in my life. I can give thanks for being me.*

FEELINGS

What you know in your head will not sustain you in moments of crisis . . . confidence comes from body awareness, knowing what you feel in the moment.
— Marion Woodman

We live in a culture that worships logical, rational, linear thought processes and disdains and ignores feelings. Feelings are seen as uncontrollable, dangerous, and unnecessary.

Yet, it is our feelings that make us human. Our feelings warn us of danger. If we are out of touch with them, we may miss danger signals.

It is our feelings, not our minds, that tell us when someone is lying to us. When we are being lied to, we feel it right in our solar plexus. We need our feelings to help us deal with the world.

———————————

MY FEELINGS *are a gift. I am lucky to have such a range of them.*

BEING PRESENT TO THE MOMENT

She would greet us pleasantly, and immediately she seemed to surround the chaotic atmosphere of morning strife with something of order, of efficient and quiet uniformity, so that one had the feeling that life was small and curiously ordered.

—Meridel LeSueur

Whew! Isn't it a relief to know that there are people in the world who are so present to the moment that when they enter a chaotic atmosphere they create calm? This calm is not born of control or manipulation. This calm is born of presence.

Only a person who is present to herself carries a feeling of serenity with her. As we work the Twelve-Step Program, we begin to experience this kind of serenity for ourselves.

———————

ORDER *that comes out of control is full of tension. Order that comes out of rigidity is full of strife. Order that comes out of serenity is peaceful.*

BUSYNESS/LONELINESS

You can get lonesome—being that busy.
                                          —Isabel Lennart

Workaholics are lonely people. Our work is like a jealous lover. It demands more and more of us. We see ourselves becoming progressively isolated from those who are important to us. We schedule lunches two weeks in advance so that we can keep up social contact with friends and then have to break or postpone these lunches because "something has come up." We get "antsy" if we are interrupted; we get irritable if someone stops by to talk because we want to get back to our work. We often don't know we are lonely because we don't stop long enough to let ourselves know what we are feeling.

———————————

IT IS GOOD *to be productive, and busyness is no substitute for intimacy.*

INTIMACY

So instant intimacy was too often followed by disillusion.

—May Sarton

We live in an age of instant dinners, instant success, and instant intimacy. We expect ourselves to meet someone and know immediately that we were meant for each other. After all, in our busy lives we don't have the time for long, drawn-out courtships.

Instant intimacy is one of the characteristics of addictive relationships. In fact, when recovering women experience a bit of instant intimacy, they have learned to run for the hills. This kind of instant connection usually does not wear well.

Intimacy takes time. It is a process. It needs to be fed, valued, nurtured, and allowed to grow. When we try to manipulate intimacy, we kill it. In fact, we often use instant intimacy to avoid the possibility of real intimacy.

———————————

INTIMACY *takes time. If I don't have time, I probably won't have intimacy.*

ANGUISH

Each woman is being made to feel it is her own cross to bear if she can't be the perfect clone of the male superman and the perfect clone of the feminine mystique.

—Betty Friedan

No wonder we sometimes find ourselves filled with anguish. There is just too much to do. Too many demands are made upon us. We are asked to be too many people—some of whom we are and some of whom we are not. Anguish is probably a normal response to such a situation.

Luckily, we do not have to stop with anguish. It is important to feel our anguish, go through it, and move on. One of the ways we stay stuck is to block our feelings and refuse to admit them. Sometimes life presents us with vises, puts us in them, and screws them tight. Then we find that as we let ourselves feel our feelings of hurt and anguish, we can move on.

———————————

A VISE *is something like a girdle: We can step out of it.*

LOVE

I wish I'd a knowed more people. I would of loved 'em all. If I'd a knowed more, I woulda loved more.
—Toni Morrison

We all have an infinite capacity for loving. Sometimes we get confused about loving, and we start thinking that we only have so much to go around. We start thinking in zero-sum terms. We believe that we only have so much love and if we give some away, we have that much less. We start parceling out our love like we pay the bills at the end of the month. We meet all of our "love obligations," and we try to keep a little bit in savings, just in case of an emergency. Controlled love is not loving. Obligatory love is not loving. Love is something that flows out of our deep sense of loving ourselves. It is not possible to love another if we don't know and love ourselves.

When we love ourselves, there is no limit to the amount of love we can share. But loving can never be manufactured because we should, need to, or want to get something in return. Love is an energy that is shared because we have it.

———————————

LOVING *the people I know allows me to know the people I love.*

PARENTING

The thing about having a baby is that thereafter you have it.

—Jean Kerr

What a shock! Our children do not always fit into our fantasies. They do not always provide us with the "perfect little family." They do not always fit in with our schemes and plans. And the worst thing about them is that we simply cannot get them shaped up the way we want them and expect them to stay that way.

When we give birth to a child, we give birth to a process that continues in one form or another for the rest of our lives. Somehow, we seemed to have missed the concept that parenting is an intimate interactive process that continues.

———————

WHEN WE STOP *trying to make our children fit our fantasies of who they* should *be, we can begin to see who they are!*

RESPONSIBILITY/GUILT

If you believe you are to blame for everything that goes wrong, you are going to stay until you fix it.
　　　　　　　　　—Susan Forward

We women who do too much are *responsible*. That is one of our great virtues, or so we think. We are willing to take accountability and blame for *everything*. When something happens at work, it must be our fault. If our relationships fail, we must have done something wrong. If our children have difficulties, we are to blame. Guilt and blame are old familiar friends. It is inconceivable to us that we did not cause . . . whatever. This is one form of our self-centeredness. We put ourselves right squarely in the middle of any disaster. Of course, the other side of the dualism is to be totally blameless and a victim. We bounce back and forth between the two.

What a difference it is to move into respondability, a place where accountability and blame have no meaning and our ability to respond is the key.

———————

MY ABILITY *to respond is hampered by accountability and blame.*

ANGER

*I am a woman in the prime of life, with certain powers
and those powers severely limited by authorities whose
faces I rarely see.*

—Adrienne Rich

It is time! As women we have been limited as to what
we can do, say, think, and feel. Some of us hate to
admit it. Yet, down deep we know that there are many
forces that limit our lives, forces over which we have
little power. Only a person with no feelings and no
awareness would not feel the smolder of anger, even
rage, deep inside at times.

It seems that we, as women, have only had two options—to go along with the authorities and thus support them, or to fight them and thus support them.
Either way we lose.

Fortunately, there is a third option. We can be ourselves. We can see what is important for us and do it.
In order for us to exercise this third option, we may
have to go through our anger first.

WHEN WE RESPECT *our anger and deal with it, we
discover doors that were not obvious before.*

ASKING FOR HELP

Advice is what we ask for when we already know the answer but wish we didn't.

—Erica Jong

Right! Usually when we ask for advice, it is because we are already aware of the answer within us, and we do not want to heed our inner knowing. Let someone else take the rap!

Also, when we ask for advice, there is a part of us just daring anyone to give it. When they do, it takes the pressure off of us, even when we know it will not work and we will secretly reject it.

Asking for help, on the other hand, is a completely different matter. Most women who do too much have great difficulty asking for help. We usually can do it ourselves, whatever "it" is, and are more comfortable doing it ourselves. We can give orders and *tell* others to do what needs to be done. We can organize and supervise. We have learned many ways of getting help without asking for it and without admitting we need it. Yet, there is something infinitely more honest in asking for help when we need it.

───────────

ASKING FOR HELP *does not mean that we are weak or incompetent. It usually indicates an advanced level of honesty and intelligence.*

AWARENESS

I felt like I was in a fog. I knew that I was desperately searching for something of great importance, the loss of which was life-threatening, but I couldn't see clearly.
                                                    —Judy Ness

We keep ourselves so busy and so overworked that we do not have time to see that we are in a fog and searching for something of great importance.

We look to our work, our money, or our families to fulfill us, and all these "solutions" fail miserably.

Even if we are successful, when we stop long enough we are aware of a feeling of loneliness and emptiness. We have failed to realize that nothing from outside can really fill us up and that the person we really long to find is ourselves. Not having ourselves and not being in touch with ourselves is life-threatening. When we leave ourselves, we are more vulnerable to outside influences and less aware of what we really need.

How exciting it is to begin to see the fog lift and to know that for which we so desperately search has been there within us all the time.

———————————

WHAT *I am looking for is not "out there." It is in me. It is me.*

ONE DAY AT A TIME/
TRUST/CONTROL

*Living is a form of not being sure, not knowing what
next or how. The moment you know how, you begin to
die a little. The artist never entirely knows. We guess.
We may be wrong, but we take leap after leap in the
dark.*

——Agnes de Mille

How arrogant *and* ignorant of us to believe that we
can do anything but live one day at a time! We are so
deluded by our illusion of control that we really believe that we can control the future, make things happen the way we want and completely control our lives.
When we do this, we cease living.

Living fully is living a life of faith. We do our foot-
work, make our plans, and then let go. Living fully is
taking a leap of faith and, before our feet are squarely
on the ground, leaping again. When we think we have
things under control, we "begin to die a little."

———

IT TAKES *a lot of faith to live one day at a time, and
the alternatives don't look that inviting.*

UNWORTHINESS/CHOICES

*The strongest lesson my mother gave me is that you are
not worthwhile if you are not doing.*

—Ferrand

Addiction to work is not something that crops up suddenly in mid-life. The seeds have often been sown in
our childhoods, and we are only living out the rules
and expectations that our parents instilled in us.

How many of our parents really believed that idle-
ness is the devil's workshop and that if they did not
keep us constantly busy, there was no telling what we
would get into? How many of us are really afraid of
idle, quiet time when nothing is on the schedule?

One mayor of a large midwest city publicly stated
that if he looked at his calendar and Tuesday night was
free, he immediately thought that his staff had goofed.
He also stated that his workaholism had ruined his
marriage and his health.

ISN'T IT EXCITING *to know that we do not have to
live out our childhood messages? As adults, we have
choices.*

BEING PRESENT TO THE MOMENT

Nobility of character manifests itself at loopholes when it is not provided with large doors.
—Mary Wilkins Freeman

Opportunities do not always come at the time or in the form we had hoped. Instead of blinding flashes of light, they are often still small voices that whisper to us in unexpected moments.

Our potential for greatness is linked with our ability to be present to the moment. Noticing may be one of the most important skills we have. When we are present to notice a small, obscure opportunity, we may discover that we have taken a major turn on the path of our life.

———————

ANYBODY *can walk through a wide-open door. I hope for the nobility of character to see the loophole.*

CONFLICT

It's better to be a lion for a day than a sheep all your life.

—Elizabeth Henry

Conflict is inevitable in our lives. We feel conflicted over a choice we must make, and the conflict is within. We feel strongly about the way a business decision must go, and we are in conflict with our peers.

Some of us believe that there are only two options when conflict arises. We must either roar like a lion and impose our will or back off like a sheep and give in (and *subtly* try to impose our will). Neither choice has much to say for it.

Thank goodness we have another option. We can check out what is going on inside of us. We can listen to what others are saying. We can get clear with ourselves and see what we have to learn.

———————————

CONFLICT *is inevitable. Fighting is a choice.*

CONNECTEDNESS/CONFUSION/
LONELINESS

*Women who set a low value on themselves make life
hard for all women.*

—Nellie McClung

As women we have a special connectedness with each
other. We have been raised to be competitive with
other women and to see them as enemies and competitors. We have also been raised to see female as inferior and told that if we wanted to get ahead, we
needed to identify with men and either become like
them or be what they wanted us to be. It has all been
very confusing. Frequently, we have felt alone and isolated.

A major factor in our healing has been to recognize
that we are women and to seek connectedness with
other women. We find ourselves reflected in their stories, and our loneliness changes to connectedness.

———————————

I AM NOT ALONE. *Other women share my experiences. Healing and connectedness are the same.*

CONTROL/ARROGANCE

The passion for setting people right is in itself an afflictive disease.

—Marianne Moore

Women who do too much often think that it is our job to set others right. After much gathering of information and acquisition of knowledge, we really have come to believe that we can and do know what is best for other people. Since we know what is best, we have no difficulty sharing this important information with any who will—or sometimes even will not—listen. Some of us even get *paid* for knowing what is best for others and setting them right.

Ugh, it doesn't look so good on paper, does it?

———————————

PERHAPS TODAY *would be a good day to look at my arrogance. Benevolent arrogance is still arrogance.*

HOPES AND DREAMS

As long as we think dugout canoes are the only possibility—all that is real or can be real—we will never see the ship, we will never feel the wind blow.
                                                    —Sonia Johnson

Women who do too much have grown afraid to dream. We know how to lust—after power, after money, after security, after relationships—but we have forgotten how to dream.

Dreaming is not limited to the unreal. Dreaming is stretching the real beyond the limits of the present. Dreaming is not being bound by the merely possible. Dreaming is not safe for our illusion of control and it is *infinitely* safe for our soul.

When we deprive ourselves of our hopes and dreams, we relegate ourselves to keeping our eyes to the ground, carefully calculating every step, and missing the pictures in the clouds and the double rainbows.

———————————

TO HOPE *and dream is not to ignore the practical. It is to dress it in colors and rainbows.*

HEALING

*The human heart does not stay away too long from
that which hurt it most. There is a return journey to
anguish that few of us are released from making.*
— Lillian Smith

Those hurts and pains that we experience in childhood don't just magically evaporate as we grow older.
They rumble around in us, and when we have reached
a level of strength, maturity, insight, and awareness to
handle them, they come up to be worked through.
This is one of the ways our inner being is loving to us.
It gives us every opportunity to heal the hurts that we
need to heal, and it gives us that opportunity when
we are strong enough to handle it.

Frequently, as children, we have experiences that
we simply aren't strong enough to handle without a
lot of support and help, and often that support is absent. So we push them down and we wait. When we
are ready, they come back up. This gives us the chance
to work through these old anguishes when we have
what we need for this task.

———————————

WHEN I AM READY, *I will have the opportunity to
make these journeys to old hurts with the knowledge
that I can heal them and move on.*

LIVING LIFE FULLY

And reach for our lives . . . for all life . . . deep into the cosmos that is our own souls.
                                            —Sonia Johnson

Each of us is a cosmos unto ourselves. When we are living our lives fully, we are separate persons, and we are also one with the universe. We are ourselves with our boundaries, and we are also connected with all things.

Luckily, we are not really asked to live any one else's life. All we have to do is live our own, and that seems to be quite enough for us.

When we live life fully, we allow ourselves to taste the range of our experiences. We see what we see, feel what we feel, and know what we know. We accept every opportunity to live out of our own souls.

———————

LUCKILY, *living life fully is not a task. It is an opportunity.*

AWARENESS OF PROCESS

He was teaching me something about flow, about choosing the right moment for everything, about enjoying the present.

—Robyn Davidson

Sometimes our teachers appear in the most unlikely forms. Robyn Davidson is speaking of an old Aborigine who traveled with her for a while. Although their cultures were vastly different, he taught her some elemental wisdom that needed to be acknowledged and experienced in her culture.

We all need to know about flow. Nothing gets done at once even when we demand it. Work and living flow in a series of nonlinear events.

Timing is also very important. We cannot correct and edit a report until it is written. When our boss is having a bad day, it is not a good idea to bring up an interpersonal problem that happened last week. We cannot control another's reactions by choosing "the right moment," and we can choose the time that is best for us. And we always have the choice to stop and enjoy the present.

———————————

WHEN I STAY *in my present, I have the opportunity to experience the flow of my life.*

BUSYNESS/EXHAUSTION/SLEEP

I am so keyed up I can't go to sleep at night. I just can't relax. I'm lucky if I get five hours of sleep a night.

—Barbie

One of the side effects of our lives as women who do too much is that we get ourselves so keyed up that we cannot get the rest and sleep we so desperately need. We are constantly on the run. Even when our bodies are ready to drop from exhaustion, we cannot relax and let them experience the soothing regeneration of deep sleep. Sometimes, even when we try to let down, it is too painful to let go, and we find we cannot. We are deprived of the healing that occurs in the alpha phase of sleep. We travel on nerves worn ragged like socks that have not been mended by caring hands. We have deprived ourselves of the unconscious experience of pulling together the tattered and torn threads of our souls and reweaving the holes gouged out by the civility of daily skirmishes. We need our rest.

———————————————

SLEEP *is one of the regenerative gifts of life. I only miss it when I don't have it.*

RUSHING/FRANTIC/UNWORTHY

My pattern is go, go, go . . . collapse.

—Rosie

When we are addicted to working, being busy, rushing around, and taking care of other people, the only way that we can give ourselves permission to rest is by collapsing.

It has been said that workaholism is the addiction of choice for those who feel unworthy. We are so driven to prove ourselves and to make a place for ourselves that we can never quite do enough, no matter how much we do. If we just do enough, maybe we can justify our existence. We have trouble accepting that just our being may be enough.

We all need solitude, and those of us who do too much can only justify taking it when we are near collapse.

Rushing and then collapsing is not only exhausting to me, it wears everyone around me out too.

———————————

RUSHING *and collapsing is cruel and inhuman behavior. Practicing it on myself is cruel and inhuman.*

SHAME

No one can make you feel inferior without your consent.

—Eleanor Roosevelt

Shame is a learned response. There is a lot of interest in shame these days in relation to addiction and recovery from addiction. When we start feeling shameful, we leave ourselves and operate much like someone on drugs or alcohol. Nothing clear can get in. Nothing clear can come out.

It is important to remember that shame is learned and that anything that is learned can be unlearned. Shame was used to control us when we were younger, and now we often use it to control others. When we start feeling ashamed, no new information can come in, we cannot process information clearly, and we cannot communicate clearly. We are in our addictive disease.

IT IS IMPORTANT *to see the role shame has played in our lives. It is also important not to stay stuck in it.*

ACCEPTANCE

It is in the knowledge of the genuine conditions of our lives that we must draw our strength to live and our reasons for living.

—Simone de Beauvoir

What a beautiful expression of the profundity of acceptance of our lives! Sometimes we are so busy rushing around that we do not take the time simply to accept who we are and what we have. Paradoxically, it is in that full acceptance that our lives then move on.

Our lives do have meaning . . . just as they are. It is our illusions that rob us of meaning, not our reality. When I accept my reality, I claim my strength and reasons for living.

———————————

MY LIFE *is what it is. It may change, and right now it is what it is.*

FREEDOM

We have not owned our freedom long enough to know exactly how it should be used.
—Phyllis McGinley

As we women have struggled to become free, we have tried out various forms of freedom. We used to think we were free when we were the kind of women men wanted us to be. Then we thought we were free when we could be like men. We thought we were free when we could treat men the way we had been treated.

We thought we were free when we had access to jobs where we could reduce our life span through stress-related diseases. We thought we were free when we had made the team and were allowed to play games in which we had no interest. We thought we were free when we had money, power, and influence.

———————

IT TAKES TIME *to grow into freedom. We have time yet.*

BUSYNESS/HOUSEWORK

There are days when housework seems the only outlet.
—Adrienne Rich

One of the comforting qualities about housework is that it is always there. When we feel at a loss for something to feed our need for busyness, we can always plunge in to housework. For some of us that means we have to be pretty desperate. In this regard the workaholic is comparable to the alcoholic who prefers a good scotch and will settle for a beer in a pinch.

It is hard for us to admit how addicted we have become to keeping busy. Our busyness affords the same numbed-out state that others get on drugs. Some of us go for the adrenaline high just as a drug addict goes for a drug high. Let's face it: we are hooked.

WHAT A RELIEF *to admit I am addicted to my busyness! Now I know recovery is possible!*

June 3

EXHAUSTION

You white people are so strange. We think it is very primitive for a child to have only two parents.
——Australian Aboriginal Elder

Past generations had the luxury and support of extended families. Grandparents were around and often found meaning in sharing stories about their life and times. As children sat listening, their parents felt the warm glow of recognition and familiarity and chuckled inwardly as old tales were told and retold.

But now many of us are isolated from extended family, or we don't have the time for family. We are it for our children. We have to be past, present, and guides to the future. This is exhausting.

———————

IN HAWAII, *people always take time to "talk story." We can learn something from them.*

GOALS

We were brought up with the value that as we sow, so shall we reap. We discarded the idea that anything we did was its own reward.

—Janet Harris

We live in a goal-oriented society. We are often so busy trying to get to the top of the mountain that we forget to notice the rocks with lichen, the alpine flowers, and even the people along the way. We are ruled by the cult of the orgasm. Foreplay is only a means to an end. Yet for many women the touching, holding, talking, stroking, and intimacy are equally if not more important that the moment of orgasm. Orgasms and goals can be fun, but not if they obliterate everything that goes before.

Setting goals can be useful and important, especially if we are willing to let them go when they become irrelevant, and if we remember that the journey itself is important.

IF I LOOK *only at the top of the mountain, I may miss the fossils along the mountainside that can teach me about time and my place in the universe.*

BEING IN CHARGE

Never retract, never explain, never apologize . . . get the thing done and let them howl.
                                        —Nellie McClery

There are so many levels on which one could respond to this quote. At one level, it sounds like advice on how to be a bulldozer and run down anyone who offers opposition. I don't recommend that.

At another level, one can zero in on the time lost in explaining, retracting, and apologizing, while the house is burning down. There is something to be said for just moving ahead.

And at another level, when we clearly feel the direction we must take and the job we must get done, there is a certain serenity that emerges when we are truly willing to "let them howl."

HOW WONDERFUL *that every issue has so many levels of truth. That makes life anything but dull.*

BELIEF: STEP ELEVEN

*I'll bet you when you get down on them rusty knees
and get to worrying God, He goes in his privy-house
and slams the door. That's what he thinks about you
and your prayers.*

— Zora Neale Hurston

Many of us who do too much have long since forsaken
our childhood "God" and have found nothing to replace "Him." When we have called upon "Him," we
were sure that he went "into his privy-house" and
slammed the door. The sound of that door slamming
has echoed and careened throughout our aloneness.
We were on our own now. We had to do it ourselves.
How dualistic we have been. If the God of our childhood didn't work, we would have no contact with any
spirituality. Yet, the real loss is our loss of contact
with our spiritual selves. We do need time for prayer,
meditation, and reflection that is congruent with who
we are. When we take that time, we find there is
something there beyond ourselves.

BELIEF *is not always easy for me. Most of all, my
thinking gets in the way.*

June 7

CAUSES/LOVE

*Those who serve a cause are not those who love that
cause. They are those who love the life which has to be
led in order to serve it . . . except in the case of the
very purest, and they are rare.*

—Simone Weil

To care about something is to bring ourselves to it.
When we give ourselves up for something, whether it
be our families, our work, our church, or our causes,
we bring an empty shell.

We have confused so much of our religious training
to mean that if we are pure, we will have no person,
no self. What most spiritual disciplines advocate is the
need to let the ego go, the need to let go of the addictive self, the need to recognize our unique oneness
with all things. When we love a cause and bring ourselves to it, we bring the very best we have.

LEARNING *to access my true self and my oneness
with all things allows me to love.*

CREATIVITY

Clutter is what silts up exactly like silt in a flowing stream when the current, the free flow of the mind, is held up by an obstruction.

—May Sarton

Clutter seems like a constant in our lives. Our houses are cluttered, our desks are cluttered, our minds are cluttered, and our lives are cluttered. This is the curse of women who do too much.

We can never find our creative selves unless we reduce some of the clutter in our lives. The mind must have the opportunity to flow freely if we are to be healthy.

We are such strong, powerful, beautiful, and intelligent women. The world needs what we have to offer.

———————————

RECOVERY *is like a dredge clearing a silted stream.*

COMPETITION/COMPARISON

*It's them that takes advantage that gets advantage i'
this world.*

—George Eliot

Unfortunately, we have been taught that to get ahead
one has to compare, compete, and take advantage of
others. And we see evidence of these behaviors all
around us.

Yet as we begin to recover from our addictions, we
begin to see that comparison and competition are both
forms of external referencing. When we compare, we
become jealous, feel bad about ourselves, find ourselves becoming resentful, and end up not liking ourselves much. When we compete, we treat others as
objects, become ruthless, and justify our destructive
behavior. When we take advantage of others, we lose
the opportunity of relationships, we become people we
do not really like, and ultimately we lose. Any of these
behaviors threatens our serenity and our recovery.

WE CONTINUE *to learn what it means to be willing
to put our sobriety first. It's not always easy and it's a
matter of life.*

SATISFACTION

Notwithstanding the poverty of my outside experience,
I have always had a significance for myself, and every
chance to stumble along my straight and narrow little
path, and to worship at the feet of my Deity, and what
more can a human soul ask for?

—Alice Jones

Satisfaction with one's life is like being anointed with warm oil. It is so peaceful to read the words of someone who is content. Often we equate contentment and satisfaction with stagnation. They are anything but that! True satisfaction with one's life is an acceptance of what is, continuing to prepare for what can be, while letting go of what we thought needed to be.

Satisfaction is an active place of quietude, a busy place of stillness. Satisfaction is a relief in living rarely felt by women who do too much. Satisfaction is the soul breathing a sigh of relief.

———————————

SOMETIMES, *when I take stock, I only look at what isn't done. I also need to look at what I have, what's been done, and what's being done.*

June 11

BEAUTY

Adornment is never anything except a reflection of the heart.

—Coco Chanel

Everyone pays so much attention to how women dress: "We should wear three-piece suits, look just like men, and dress for success." "Women who get raped were asking for it by the way they dressed." "Men like women who dress in a feminine fashion. It makes men feel masculine."

Is it any wonder that we sometimes feel confused about what seems right for us to wear?

What if the way we dress is simply a reflection of our hearts? What if our main criterion for beauty is what feels good on our bodies and reflects who we are? What if we wear colors because we like them and not because they are "our colors" or make us look thin? This opens up all kinds of possibilities, doesn't it?

IF I ADORNED MYSELF *to reflect my heart, what would I wear?*

Self-Awareness

Men look at themselves in mirrors. Women look for themselves.

—Elissa Melamed

"Mirror, mirror, on the wall" . . . where did I go? It seems only yesterday that when I looked in the mirror I saw someone I recognized. Those little pieces of myself that I gave away one by one seemed so insignificant at the time. What has become of me?

So many of us who do too much have the experience of disappearing before our very eyes. We did not plan it that way. It just seemed to happen over the years.

Yet, if there is still someone to look in the mirror, we have not left completely.

———————

I NEED to look closely. The mirror could be my friend. It could help lead me back to me.

LIVING LIFE FULLY/CURIOSITY

Life was meant to be lived and curiosity must be kept alive. One must never, for whatever reason, turn his [sic] back on life.

—Eleanor Roosevelt

As I look back over the significant teachers in my life, one of the characteristics that consistently stands out is their curiosity. We sometimes think that curiosity is reserved for youth and is only natural in young children.

Yet I am sure that if we think about the people we have known, those that we remember most vividly are those who remained incurably curious throughout their lives.

There is an intimate link between curiosity and aliveness. Curiosity appears to be in the gene bank of the human species. My curiosity is not dead, even though it may seem to have been slumbering for a while.

MAY I NEVER BE *"cured" of my curiosity!*

AWARENESS OF PROCESS/WISDOM

The events in our lives happen in a sequence in time, but in their significance to ourselves, they find their own order . . . the continuous thread of revelation.
                                        —Eudora Welty

Wouldn't it be boring if our lives were completely linear? How dull to have completely worked through each experience and trauma right when it happened!

Yet we all become resentful when old skeletons that we believed were long since buried begin to rattle their bones. How inconvenient when the effects of events that happened at age five begin to erupt at age thirty-five! How disquieting when memories long hidden from consciousness signal us that they are ready to be worked through!

Can we believe that our own inner process knows when we are ready to deal with old issues? Can we trust that the very fact that they are coming up is an indication of how much we have grown and how strong we are?

———————————

THERE IS SOMETHING *within me that knows more than I know. Trusting it can only result in healing.*

CONFUSION/NEGATIVISM

Why is it when I don't know I want, there is always someone waiting to tell me what it is? I'm just lucky, I guess.

—Anne Wilson Schaef

I have heard so many women say, "I have a good marriage. My husband doesn't beat me, he doesn't gamble, and he doesn't run around with other women." Or they say, "Well, my job isn't boring, it keeps me busy, and it pays the bills." Somehow, OK becomes the absence of awful. If something in our lives isn't too destructive, it must be all right.

We get so confused about what we really want and what is really good for us. We are so accustomed to doing what is expected of us that we have lost our ability to determine what we want.

———————————

UNLESS I KNOW *what I want and what is right for me, there is no way I can be an honest person.*

CONTROL

War is the unfolding of miscalculations.
                                        —Barbara Tuchman

We are so invested in the illusion of control that we rarely step back and see how pervasive and destructive this illusion is. Much of what goes on at an international level between nations is based upon the illusion of control. When we believe we can control everything or we have everything under control, we are appalled by our miscalculations. Miscalculations on a personal level can be just as devastating as miscalculations on an international level. It is not the *mis* in miscalculating that is the problem; it is the calculating. When we operate out of a belief system that says that we should be able to understand everything and that when we do we can control everything, we are in big trouble.

WARS *are disastrous whether they are within me, between individuals, or between countries.*

SELF-AWARENESS

*I want to find out who I am and give up letting every-
one else define me.*

—Judith

As women, we have been trained to look for our identity outside ourselves. We have been raised to be
someone's daughter, someone's wife or partner, and
someone's mother. What others think of us has been
who we are. Even when we are successful professional
women, we find ourselves looking outside for identity
and validation. This habit is embedded deep in the
marrow of our bones even when we look strong and
self-defined.

An important part of our recovery is finding out
who we *really* are—not who we have been *told* we
should be, not who we *think* we should be, and not
who we image ourselves to be.

Who is this person I call me? She has the potential
of being one of the most interesting persons I have
ever met. Yet, I hardly know her.

———————

TODAY *I have the opportunity to begin or continue
an inner journey that can last the rest of my life.*

LIVING IN THE PRESENT

I know the solution. When we have a world of only now with no shadows of yesterdays or clouds of tomorrow, then saying what we can do will work.
                    —Goldie Ivener

Imagine starting each day fresh with no "shadows of yesterdays or clouds of tomorrow." In our more negative, cynical moods, we hear such an idea and we scoff, impossible! It is not possible to let go of the past and have no concern for the future. Yet this is what every great spiritual teacher on this planet has taught in one way or another. In fact, the greatest gift our spiritual teachers have given us has often been to show us how to live in the present, how to simply be totally present to the moment.

How often we miss our life by focusing on the past or yearning for the future. We miss the look in our children's eyes today, because we are thinking about how to get them to the dentist tomorrow. We miss the interesting idea that has just now come across our desk, because we are worrying about what we said in the meeting yesterday. Stop—relax—be here!

THE PRESENT *is all I have: to leave it is to kill it.*

ACCEPTANCE OF SELF

*Do nothing because it is righteous or praiseworthy or
noble to do so; do nothing because it seems good to do
so; do only that which you must do and which you
cannot do in any other way.*

—Ursula K. Le Guin

We are so accustomed to doing what others want us to
do, or doing what is right, or doing that which earns us
praise, that LeGuin's words urging us to do only that
which we *must* do and cannot do in any other way
seem unrealistic. We think: That's fine for her to say,
she's a writer—she schedules her own time.

Yet, what truth is there for us in her words? We certainly can admit that we have done many things for the
wrong reasons, and the pain of our righteousness, "nobility," or praise-seeking is often bitter in our hearts.
Often when we do something because it seems good to
do so, we waste everyone's time, including our own.

What a relief to believe that we are enough just as
we are and that our unique way of accomplishing a
task is just what is needed.

———————

I WILL SIT *with these ideas. After all, who else could
make my contribution!*

EXPECTATIONS

Life's under no obligation to give us what we expect.
—Margaret Mitchell

Expectations are real killers! They are setups for disappointment. Often, because of our expectations, we are completely oblivious to what is really going on in a situation. Because we are so wedded to what we think *should* be happening, or what we want to happen, we don't see what *is* happening.

Many a possible relationship has been aborted because we were too determined to turn it into *a relationship*.

Expectations also keep us in illusion. We set up our expectations for someone, we project them onto the other person, and then we start reacting to our expectations as if they were real. Expectations and the illusion of control are intimately linked.

WHEN WE *are tied to our expectations we usually miss what's happening . . . life, that is.*

BEAUTY/COMPARISON

I am as my Creator made me, and since He [sic] is sat-isfied, so am I.

—Minnie Smith

How beautiful and how simple it is just to accept our-selves the way we are. Women, especially, have diffi-culty simply seeing the beauty in who we are. We are always comparing ourselves to others: no matter what we have or who we are, it never quite seems to be enough. We are always too much or too little, too fat or too skinny, too intelligent or not intelligent enough, too aggressive or not assertive enough. Whenever we compare ourselves to others, we lose.

The very act of comparison is part of the problem. Comparison is one of the processes of addiction. In that process, we leave ourselves and lose ourselves. There are other options.

———————

IMAGINE *a day*—today *for example*—*of just being satisfied with who I am.*

AWARENESS OF PROCESS

*Life comes in clusters, clusters of solitude, then clusters
when there is hardly time to breathe.*
                                          —May Sarton

We workaholics, busyaholics, and rushaholics feel
much more familiar with and comfortable with times
when we hardly have time to breathe. We know how
to function under pressure and with deadlines hover-
ing over us. These times are when we shine.

Unfortunately, it is the time of calm and potential
solitude after the project is finished that scares us. To
be without a project or a deadline strikes terror in
our bones. Fortunately, we rarely have to deal with
that terror because we have arranged our lives in such
a way as to rarely have a "breather."

If we take time to notice, this ebb and flow in life has
a reason. We need breathers. Our bodies need to rest
from our constant adrenaline push, or they blow up.

As we let ourselves get healthier, we begin to experience and treasure the "clusters" of our lives and welcome them as examples of infinite wisdom.

THE OCEAN *never tires of the ebb and flow of the
tides. I have something to learn from the ocean.*

June 23

AWARENESS

In contemporary America people are again discovering how to drink from their own wells.
—Lynn R. Laurence

Part of our disease is looking outside ourselves for someone who will fix our lives for us. We sometimes even believe that God or a power greater than ourselves can make everything all right—that we just have to sit back and let it happen. Not so.

When we recognize that the force we believed to be outside of ourselves is indeed within us—then we begin to heal. Healing is the experience of the oneness of all things and our ability to take our place in that oneness.

As a society, our "other-directedness" has been destructive. Changing to "me-ness" and self-centeredness has not helped much either. Recognizing that we are one with all things and accepting our place in that oneness moves us into and beyond ourselves.

MY THIRST *can only be quenched from my own well and my awareness that this well is mine and is shared by all.*

COURAGE

This is the art of courage: to see things as they are and still believe that the victory lies not with those who avoid the bad, but those who taste, in living awareness, every drop of the good.

—Victoria Lincoln

How aptly put! Courage is not just seeing things as they are, which is vastly important, courage is accepting reality with the ingenuity to continue to see and experience the many good things that happen to us.

I remember in graduate school I acquired the nickname "Pollyanna," because I always could see something interesting and exciting in everything that happened. I did not always like those grueling reports and seemingly sadistic examinations and yet, when I was honest with myself, I always had to admit that I had learned something when I finished. Because of the nickname and the subtle judgmentalism attached to it, I began to question myself. After some reflection, I realized that a pollyanna was someone who denied the negative and only saw the positive. I did not do that. I saw and accepted the negative and delighted in whatever positive there was. As a consequence, graduate school was not difficult for me. Working has not been hard for me either.

A SMILE, *a nod in the elevator, a few minutes of quiet time—these are living every drop of the good.*

Unworthiness

*I switched from my negative thinking to my worka-
holism. That's how I continue to abuse myself.*

—Judy

Our feelings of unworthiness take many forms, and
one of the most obvious is self-abuse. Many women
are beginning to see that their addiction to self-abuse
is their most basic addiction.

It is abusive to the self to work too much. It is abusive to the self to keep so busy that we have no time
for ourselves. It is abusive to the self to be so busy
taking care of others that we have no awareness of our
needs. It is abusive to the self to be so externally ref-
erenced that we have lost a sense of self.

When we abuse ourselves, it is inevitable that we
will also abuse others. Both forms of abuse are destructive.

————————

ALTHOUGH *I have become inured to self-abuse, I really do not believe that it is right for me. I will try to
open myself to what is right for me.*

LIVING LIFE FULLY

When I speak of the erotic, then I speak of it as an assertion of the life force of women; of that creative energy empowered, the knowledge and use of which we are now reclaiming in our language, our history, our dancing, our loving, our work, our lives.
—Audre Lorde

What a wonderful opportunity today is to celebrate ourselves as women! To celebrate ourselves does not mean that we put men down or do not like men. We are only celebrating ourselves and the unique contribution that women have made, are making, and can make.

All of us have gifts that are unique to us. No one else has quite the combination of gifts that each of us has to offer and many of those gifts are not in spite of being a woman, they are *because* we are women. Not to share the fullness of our woman gifts is a form of stinginess, and no one likes to be stingy.

WHEE! *I celebrate me!*

June 27

ACTION

If you want a thing well done, get a couple of old broads to do it.

—Bette Davis

If there is anything we "old broads" know how to do, it is to get things done. We women are so practical. We have an uncanny ability to see what needs to be done, roll up our sleeves, and do it. We are rarely too proud, too prissy, or too elitist to do what needs to be done.

Sometimes we fail to see how important our practical everydayness is. We long for the great inspiration, the important recognition, or the big breakthrough. Yet all our lives are made up of common tasks that need to be done. When something is common and ordinary, we frequently fail to see its real importance. What we do *is* important, and we do it well. Failing to see that is a form of dishonesty. And we don't want to be dishonest, do we?

I AM *a competent "old broad." At least Bette Davis appreciated me. Maybe I can appreciate myself.*

June 28

WHOLENESS

Don't you realize that the sea is the home of water? All water is off on a journey unless it's in the sea, and it's homesick, and bound to make its way home someday.
— Zora Neale Hurston

We are all like water. We are off on a journey to return to ourselves. Some of our journeys have taken us far afield, and many of our days have been absorbed by the sandy river banks that contain us. Yet we continue to flow—heavy and swollen in the spring of our lives and often reduced to a trickle as we approach the fall of our years. "Return, return, return," we murmur, as we tumble over the stones in our paths, ever cognizant that although we may wander through new and strange lands, our destination is a return.

WATER *has to return to the sea, just as I have to return to me.*

SELF-AFFIRMATION/POWER

*Think of yourself as an incandescent power, illuminated
perhaps and forever talked to by God and his [sic] mes-
sengers.*

—Brenda Ueland

As we begin to get more in touch with ourselves and
accept ourselves for who we are, we begin to enter-
tain the thought that we might, indeed, be "an incandescent power." We begin to feel our power and know
it not as power over others, but as personal power,
glowing within.

As we clear out the garbage of our crazy addictive
behavior, we uncover a spiritual being lying dormant,
not dead, within us. We have a sense of what it means
to be in tune with the infinite, and life feels easy and
flowing. This feeling of oneness is not an illusion; it
is real. Only as we learn to affirm who we are do we
move beyond ourselves.

AS WE AFFIRM *who we are, we become who we are.*

June 30

RECOVERY
STEP ONE

Recovery is a process, not an event.
— Anne Wilson Schaef

Now that we are beginning to recognize that over-working, caretaking, rushing around, and always keeping busy are manifestations of the addictive process and are just as much a disease as chemical addictions, we want to stop this immediately. Unfortunately, it is not that easy. The very definition of an addiction or compulsive behavior is something that has us in its grip over which we are powerless. We can't "just say no." We can't just stop what we are doing. This disease is in the cells of our muscles and in the marrow of our bones.

We need to realize that recovery is a process. It took time for us to get this way, and it takes time for us to recover. Part of our disease is wanting everything to happen at once. We need patience with ourselves and support from others to progress in our recovery process.

───────────────

"I HAVE *to do it [recovery] myself; I don't have to do it alone," are statements often heard in recovery circles.*

NICENESS

I haven't been being nice . . . I've been chicken.
—Claudia

As women we have been trained to be nice. We *do* "nice" things for people, we *say* "nice" things, and we *are* "nice." Many of us fear that if we stop being nice, we have to become nasty. Having become bored with our niceness, many of us have experimented with nasty.

For those of us trying to get clearer with ourselves and others, we have discovered that our niceness is intimately linked with our dishonesty. If we want to be more honest, we have to be willing to let go of our "niceness." In letting go of our niceness, we find ourselves becoming more honest. Getting honest about ourselves and our lives is an essential step toward health. To be more honest, we also have to give up being chicken and put ourselves out there.

OFTEN, *when we say we are being nice to protect other people, the person we are really protecting is ourselves.*

LIVING LIFE FULLY

I have made a great discovery.
What I love belongs to me. Not the chairs and
tables in my house, but the masterpieces of the world.
It is only a question of loving them enough.
                                        —Elizabeth Asquith Bibesco

We get so embroiled with possessions. We find ourselves feeling that we need to own places, persons,
and things. We try to possess our lives, and we believe
that we can. We need to learn from the butterfly that
alights on our hand. If we watch it and admire it, as it
chooses to stay for a while, we are blessed with its
beauty. If we try to hold onto it, we will kill it. It is in
the not trying to possess that we have.

Imagine what it really means that we can have all
the treasures of the world—not to own, but to appreciate, to enjoy . . . to live with.

———————————

AM I *capable of loving so much that I am able to ap-*
preciate that which I do not possess? I hope so.

July 3

HUMOR

*Yo' ole black hide don't look lak nothin' tuh me, but
uh passel uh wrinkled up rubber, wid yo' big ole yeahs
flappin' on each side lak uh paih uh buzzard wings.*
—Zora Neale Hurston

I love the writing of Zora Neale Hurston. She has a
way of cutting right through to the meat of things,
and she does it with humor and clarity. How often
have we had thoughts similar to those quoted above,
and we haven't let ourselves enjoy the tickle and the
giggle in our own minds? We make life so *serious* and
everything so *important* that we don't dare laugh—it
might offend. We might offend.

In order not to offend, we render ourselves and our
lives humorless. How dull.

———————

I THINK *it might be helpful to remember that our
humor adds color to a world gone grey with inatten-
tion.*

July 4

SELF-ESTEEM

*People call me a feminist whenever I express sentiments
that differentiate me from a doormat or a prostitute.*
— Rebecca West

When a woman believes that she is equal, she is called
uppity. When we stand up for what we know and for
what we believe, we are called aggressive and unfemi-
nine. When we state that women are wonderful and
that we are proud to be a woman, we are told that we
are antimale.

When we put forth our perceptions, we are told
that we don't understand reality. When we put forth
our values, we are told that we are crazy and we just
don't understand the way the world works. Is it any
wonder that we sometimes have trouble with self-esteem?

———————————

BATTERING *comes in many forms. My self-esteem is
constantly assailed, yet it's really mine when I get
right down to it.*

ISOLATION

I create my own prisons. No one else is putting these walls around me.

—Michelle

Rarely do we recognize the construction of our enclosures until they are already built. We are fooled by their illusionary appearance: they look like security, prestige, power, influence, money, and acceptance. It is only when the construction is completed that we realize that we are enclosed in splendid isolation. When did it happen? We looked down at our work or our lives for only a second, and then looked up to find that our illusions of security have become a benevolent prison. Prisons have room for fantasies, but prisons have little room for dreams.

We have misjudged our priorities. We do not want the isolation of success at any cost. Somehow, we thought we could "have it all" and now all of it has us.

———————

MY ISOLATION *has been of my making, so my reaching out for help can also be of my doing.*

July 6

FORGIVENESS/AMENDS

Her breasts and arms ached with the beauty of her own forgiveness.

—Meridel Le Sueur

To ache with my own forgiveness is to be wholly accepting of myself. None of us is without need of forgiveness. In our disease, we have all done injury to those closest to us. This is one of the most painful aspects of addictive diseases: we hurt those we love the most. We hurt ourselves when we hurt those we love. When we are preparing to make amends to others, we must first make amends to ourselves and forgive ourselves for the wrongs we have done. Only then can we be truly ready to make our amends to others.

There is, indeed, a beauty in our forgiveness of ourselves. We can be simple, direct, and without fanfare in our forgiveness of ourselves.

———————————

I AM *in need of forgiveness. I am in need of forgiveness of myself.*

July 7

FRIENDS

From the first time I met the little girl until her death recently, a period of a little over seventy years, we were friends.

—Mrs. Mary E. Ackley

"We were friends"—such a simple yet powerful statement: "We were friends." How many of us can truly say that we are a friend?

One of the devastating realities of busyness and doing too much is that we progressively have less and less time for friends.

We have to make appointments for friendship. Hanging out with a friend seems a luxury or even an inconvenience. Or we assume that we are friends and never do anything to nurture the relationship. We treat our friends like we treat ourselves, and that's not very nice.

IT IS NOT POSSIBLE *to live a rich, full life without friends. I have to be one to have one.*

GROWTH

My favorite thing is to go where I've never been.
                                        —Diane Arbus

To go where we have never been, whether internally or externally, is always exciting. This excitement may be covered over by fear and trepidation. Yet I have always found that somewhere deep inside of us we are excited when we have the opportunity to explore the unknown.

Men are not the only explorers. We women are explorers too. Our explorations may take different forms: we love to try out a new recipe; we love to try out a new idea or ideology; we love to visit new places and learn from different cultures. We are especially adept at courageously launching into hidden and unknown areas in ourselves and others. In spite of our fears, there is a deep quest for our truth in each of us.

I PREFER *a road map on my journeys, and I am willing to go without one if I must.*

Enthusiasm

One needs something to believe in, something for which one can have whole-hearted enthusiasm. One needs to feel that one's life has meaning, that one is needed in this world.

—Hannah Senesh

Several years ago, I made a drastic decision for myself. I decided that I would do only work that I was enthusiastic about. I was a psychotherapist, speaker, and workshop leader then. This decision was very frightening for me, since I was a single parent and had many financial responsibilities.

I decided not to accept any clients about whom I wasn't enthusiastic. I would not do any speeches or workshops just because of the money, or prestige, or ego. I would do only what seemed *right* for me to do. I would do only things that intuitively seemed related to the meaning and purpose of my life. I feared I would end up a derelict, a bag lady, and starve, yet, I have had more money since that decision than I ever had before. I still live my life based on that decision.

———————

I'm not saying *this will work for everybody,* and *it worked for me.*

EXHAUSTION

You came as a solemn army to bring a new life to man [sic]. You tore that life you knew nothing about out of their guts——and you told them what it had to be. You took their every hour, every minute, every nerve, every thought in the farthest corners of their souls——and you told them what it had to be. You came and you forbade life to the living.

—Ayn Rand

It sounds here as if Ayn Rand is talking about this addictive, white-male system in which we live, a system that is innately foreign to women, and one which we have come to believe that we have to learn and participate in to survive. This is not reality—it is a system, and as a system holds no more truth than any other system. Unfortunately we have been taught that it is reality, although at some level all of us know it isn't. Also, unfortunately, this system thrives on addictions and requires them in order for us to tolerate it. Fortunately, we do have other options.

———————————————

I'M TIRED *of trying to be something I'm not.*

GOALS

*It is good to have an end to journey towards; but it is
the journey that matters in the end.*
                                        —Ursula K. Le Guin

When we remember that life is a process, it helps us
put our goal-setting in perspective. The purpose of
setting goals is to give us a temporary structure in
which to operate. Unfortunately, when we begin to
believe that the structure is solid and real, we lose
touch with the process of getting there. This is why we
often feel so depressed and let down when we reach
our goals. We have not let ourselves enjoy the experience of the journey, and when we reach the end, we
have missed the journey.

Being in the present allows us to experience the
journey and to respond to the process of the journey.
When we operate this way, we see that all goals are
just temporary ideas that change as we draw near to
them.

EACH DAY *is a journey. Each day is a process.*

July 12

Guilt/Alone Time

*I wanted to drive up here alone and several people asked
if they could drive up here with me. I can't tell you how
hard it was just to come by myself.*

—Mary

Often we feel guilty when we do something for ourselves. We have so accepted the mandate to be aware
of other's feelings, take care of them, and put ourselves last that we often feel uncomfortable if we even
have needs. How selfish it seems to refuse a ride to
someone who needs it when we are going that way
anyway. Surely we could put ourselves out a little.
Even if we do refuse the request and get our time
alone, are we going to be so overcome with guilt that
we won't enjoy the time anyway? What a lose-lose situation!

Maybe we can use that time alone to explore our
gift of guilt and learn from it. Even having time to explore our guilt requires alone time. We may need that
exploration desperately.

WHEN I SAY *no to a request for my time, I am not
going away from that person, I am going to myself.*

BEING IN CHARGE

I'm not going to limit myself just because people won't accept the fact that I can do something else.
—Dolly Parton

There is a vast difference between trying to control our lives and taking charge of our lives. Trying to control our lives puts us in a position of failure before we start and causes endless, unnecessary pain and suffering.

Taking charge of our lives means owning our lives and having a respond-ability to our lives and then letting it go. Taking charge of our lives means that we do not spin our wheels with impression-management and try to be what others want us to be. It also means that we do not accept their evaluation of what we cannot be and stop there.

WHEN I LET GO *of my need to control, I am in a better position to be in charge and to receive information from my power greater than myself.*

July 14

BEING TORN

At work, you think of the children you have left at home. At home, you think of the work you've left unfinished. Such a struggle is unleashed within yourself. Your heart is rent.

—Golda Meir

Being torn seems to be an accepted given for women who run a home and also have other work. Many of us have tried to be superwomen and have almost pulled it off. Yet even when it appears that we are "making it" and successful in both arenas, we are aware that internally we feel torn and guilty in relation to our family. Frequently, this results in our taking our frustration out on our children, which results in more guilt. We feel like a violin string pulled taut and about to break.

Perhaps it is time to sit down with our families and tell them how we feel. They probably need to hear that we really *want* to be with them and that we do not know how to balance our lives. They may even feel relieved to know that our lives feel overwhelming (which everyone but us has admitted!).

JUST PLAIN HONESTY *works for so many things. Perhaps I really shouldn't just save it for special occasions.*

CREATIVITY
STEP ELEVEN

*I feel a recipe is only a theme, which an intelligent cook
can play each time with a variation.*
—Madame Benoit

It sounds so simple for creativity to find its way.

We need quiet—the word sounds familiar. We can
dimly remember times of quiet. Or was it when we
were sleeping?

And we need time—just for ourselves with no
agenda, no deadlines, no needs of others impinging
upon us.

We long for quiet and time for our themes to
emerge. Recovery is not possible without both. Contact with our Higher Power is not possible without
both.

———————————

NO ONE ELSE *will arrange any quiet time for me.
I have to see to it myself.*

BALANCE

*Creative minds have always been known to survive any
kind of bad training.*

—Anna Freud

Even though her father believed that our lives are determined in our first five years, Anna Freud seems to
have moved beyond him. Although we are affected by
our past and our training, each of us has within us the
possibility of moving beyond them.

Unfortunately, when we try *not* to be like our parents, we get caught in the same trap as when we feel
that we *have* to be like them. Either way we are determined by our past and controlled by our reaction to
our past. Some of us spend our entire lives vacillating
between these two positions.

We do have another choice. That choice is to acknowledge our past and be ourselves.

———————————

THE THIRD *option is to be me. That is where my creativity lies.*

CONTROL

With the only certainty in our daily existence being
change, and a rate of change growing always faster in
a kind of technological leapfrog game, speed helps
people think they are keeping up.

—Gail Sheehy

Our illusion of control dies very slowly. The more
changing and uncertain our lives are, the more we fall
back on our favorite illusion that if we can just get in
charge we can control everything. We have forgotten
that there is a difference between control and facili-
tating good work. Robert Blake and Jane Mouton,
management consultants, developed the concept of a
back-up style for managers. Regardless of how much
management training people have, or how intelligent
or educated they are, under stress they resort to a
back-up style, and that back-up style often is one of
trying to *control* the situation. Unfortunately, control
never works. It isn't even possible. That's one reason
we feel like such failures.

TURNING *a situation over to a Higher Power is not*
easy under stress, although that is probably when I
most need to do so.

POWERLESSNESS

I found out that I can cut my working time to fifteen hours a week and I can still do that workaholically.
—Michelle

For those of us who are workaholics, rushaholics, and busyaholics, it is almost impossible to admit that we are powerless over our disease. Slowly and often painfully we become aware that we simply *can't stop,* even when we would like to. If we are not busy doing something, we feel anxious and unworthy. We have arranged our lives around our work, and we simply cannot stop. This is powerlessness. We become progressively aware that our busyness and our working are interfering with our lives. Our lives are becoming unmanageable. There is just too much to do.

It is difficult for us to admit powerlessness, because we can do more than others and we pride ourselves in having things under control. As we become aware that our control is out of control, we may be ready to start on a path of recovering our lives.

ONLY *in acknowledging my powerlessness over my working and busyness can I begin to heal.*

July 19

ALONE TIME/BEING RESPONSIBLE

For every five well-adjusted and smoothly functioning Americans, there are two who never had the chance to discover themselves. It may well be because they have never been alone with themselves.

—Marya Mannes

Superwomen can always be heard to say, "I know that having time to oneself is important. It's just not possible for me. I just have too many responsibilities."

One always wonders how women who seem so powerful and so much on top of their lives can become so helpless in determining what they do with their time. Our helplessness seems to be situational and often emerges only in relation to *our* needs.

As successful women, we are often least successful in caring for ourselves. We need skill training in self-help.

THE CHOICES I *make about what I do with my time are* my *choices (even when they don't appear to be!).*

INTIMACY/EXCUSES: STEP ONE

Because of his need to concentrate absolutely on his work, George Sarton had developed extreme resistance to anything that might prove disturbing, such as my mother's health or lack of it.

——May Sarton

How easy it is to become so self-centered in our work that we cannot even see the needs of those closest to us! Often, our work is used as an excuse to avoid intimacy with ourselves and others. No matter what the work is, if it is "work," it is justified.

Often we ask those we love to make tremendous sacrifices in the name of our work, and we become unfeeling and uncaring in the process. It is the work that matters. Women who are addicted to their housework are just as demonic as those who are addicted to their businesses. Both can be escapes from intimacy.

Recovery offers us the possibility of intimacy with ourselves and others. However, to experience the joy of recovery we have first to admit what we are doing.

———————

INTIMACY *is like a drink of fresh water to a work-worn soul. Even a taste can bring forth desert flowers.*

AWARENESS OF PROCESS/FEAR

Now some people when they sit down to write and nothing special comes, no good ideas, are so frightened that they drink a lot of strong coffee to hurry them up, or smoke packages of cigarettes, or take drugs or get drunk. They do not know that ideas come slowly, and that the more clear, tranquil and unstimulated you are, the slower the ideas come, but the better they are.

—Brenda Ueland

One of the side effects of our addictive doing too much is that we begin to use chemicals and other addictive substances to keep us going. Then our addiction to doing too much becomes compounded with a complex array of other addictions.

Another side effect of being women who do too much is that we find ourselves progressively out of touch with our creativity and our productivity.

Brenda Ueland uses the focus of becoming a writer to call us back to ourselves. Yet, the truth in what she is saying applies not only to writers, it applies to all of us. Our creativity and productivity always suffer when we use addictive substances to try to force them.

———————————

I DON'T NEED *to* do *something for my creativity to emerge. I probably need to* stop *doing some things.*

SUCCESS

Life is a succession of moments. To live each one is to succeed.

—Corita Kent

Perhaps it is not the concept of success that is the problem, it is the way we define success. If we define success as lots of money, getting to the top of the organizational ladder, two BMWs in our garage, and a designer house, success may be dangerous to our health.

If we define success as living each successive moment to its fullest, we may have money, prestige, and possessions, and this success may *not* be disastrous to our health. The difference is in the attitude and in the beliefs behind that attitude.

In fact, it is often easier to gather the accouterments of success than it is to live a successful life. Living a successful life demands our presence, our presence in each moment.

———————

SUCCESS *gets confusing. Is it what I have or what has me? Probably neither.*

July 23

ACCEPTANCE/SELF-CONFIDENCE

One startling finding, given that these women had an average IQ of one hundred forty three, was their lack of confidence in their abilities and the belief that their intellectual selves were ephemeral or were not developed.

—Carol Tomlinson-Keasey

People have said that the women's movement is the only revolution where the outpost of the enemy is in our own minds (not that we need to think in terms of enemies). We like to think that women have overcome their negative programming and that we really do feel good about ourselves. Then we read a study like the one done by Carol Tomlinson-Keasey, and we feel a lingering sadness for a group of intelligent women who do not believe in themselves or their abilities.

We are aware that these women who mistrust themselves and their intellect are, down deep, not so different from us.

We may put up a good front, and yet we know there are still those little hidden niggling fears that maybe we just are not good enough.

I AM SAD *when women do not value themselves. I am sad when I do not value myself. I will let myself feel that sadness.*

ACCEPTANCE/HUMILITY

But if you go and ask the sea itself, what does it say?
Grumble, grumble, swish, swish. It is too busy being the
sea to say anything about itself.
                                        —Ursula K. Le Guin

No one who has ever sat beside the sea and experienced her eternal power and gentleness can have any
question that the sea knows that she is just that, the
sea. Nature has such an ability to be exactly what she
is, with no pretense . . . and she does not even have to
stop and think about it.

When we have to stop and think who we are, we
are not being who we are. When we are trying to be
someone we believe we should be, we are not being
who we are. When we are trying to be what someone
else has told us we should be, we are not being ourselves. To be myself, I have to *be*.

NATURE *teaches great lessons in humility. In order to*
learn from her, I have to be in her.

WONDER

I take a sun bath and listen to the hours, formulating, and disintegrating under the pines, and smell the resiny hardi-hood of the high noon hours. The world is lost in a blue haze of distances, and the immediate sleeps in a thin and finite sun.

—Zelda Fitzgerald

I read the above passage, and I feel lost in wonder— wonder at the beauty of the words and phrases. I read it and I remember the wonder of a spontaneous sun-bath in a light-speckled woods where the sun on my skin enhanced the mixed scent of forest musk and pungent pine, as the smells permeated my body. I can remember listening to the hours as they initially crashed around me, then gradually smoothed into a murmur as my body relaxed into the earth and into myself. The world seemed far away, and there was no need to bring it closer.

———————————

WONDER *is a gift of living. Living is a gift of wonder.*

TRUST

Nature has created us with the capacity to know God, to experience God.

—Alice Walker

We often think that we have to work to know God and that we have to have experts to teach us how to know our Higher Power.

What a wonderful surprise it is suddenly to discover that the capacity to know God and be connected with our Higher Power dwells within us and to discover that instead of working at this connection, we have only to admit that it is already there. We may have lost our awareness of our relationship with our Higher Power, and the connection has never stopped. It is only that our awareness of it has dimmed and become obscure.

———————————

I HAVE *all I need within me to know and experience my Higher Power. All I have to do is step out of my way.*

PERFECTIONISM/LONELINESS

> "She happens to belong to a type [of American woman]
> I frequently met . . . it goes to lectures. And entertains
> afterwards . . . , amazing, their energy," he went on.
> "They're perfectly capable of having three or four chil-
> dren, running a house, keeping abreast of art, litera-
> ture and music—superficially of course, but good Lord,
> that's something—and holding down a job into the
> bargain. Some of them get through two or three hus-
> bands as well, just to avoid stagnation."
>
> —Dodie Smith

It sort of grates to see ourselves described on paper.
We have learned to cope. We have learned to be superwomen. So what if we don't go very deeply into
anything. How can we? We just don't have the time.
Our biggest fear is not knowing enough or not being
enough. We feel that we are inadequate if we cannot
talk intelligently about almost everything and do almost anything. We would like to have more intimate
relationships, but we just do not have the time—we
are perfect women.

———————

WE ARE *perfect women, and being perfect is boring
to ourselves and others.*

REALITY/DENIAL

We flood our minds with words! They mesmerize and manipulate us, masking the truth even when it's set down squarely in front of us. To discover the underlying reality, I've learned to listen only to the action.
— Judith M. Knowlton

Letting go of our ability to discern reality is one of the characteristics of addiction. As well-known psychotherapist Marion Woodman says, "In addiction you create a fantasy and try and live there." So often we women who do too much are gullible on a very deep level. We *want* to believe what others tell us, and we do not want to have to be on our toes all the time. As a result, we often feel resentful and sad because we find ourselves dealing with illusion and not reality. It's not that we don't perceive reality. We do. We just don't want to have to deal with it. We would rather complain and be hurt. We can always see reality when we take off our filters. And reality is always easier to deal with than fantasy in the long run.

———————

ACTIONS *do speak louder than words, and when I believe what others* do *and do not listen so much to what they say, I feel saner.*

INTEGRITY

> *Tell me*
> > *Mother*
> > > *What has taken your soul*
> > > *away*
> > > > *so cruelly?*

—Chungmi Kim

One of the effects of an addictive disease is that it destroys our integrity. We see ourselves doing things at work that compromise our value system, and we say nothing. We are reprimanded for something for which we were not responsible, and we say nothing. We act in ways that are not in keeping with our own personal morality.

The addiction to doing too much is just like any other addiction in that it puts us in a position where we are willing to do anything to get our "adrenaline buzz," to get our "fix." We see ourselves participating in decisions that are wrong for us, we neglect ourselves, and we neglect our families. We have lost our integrity.

WHEN I *lose my integrity, I, like Chungmi Kim's Mother, have lost (or at least misplaced) my soul.*

CONTRADICTIONS

*If I could see what's going on with myself as well as I
see what's going on with others, I'd be "fixed" by now.*
—Pat

So much of our lives are glaring contradictions. We
swear that we will never be like our mothers, then
find ourselves screeching on the same note. We know
we would never manipulate others the way our boss
manipulates us, and then we catch ourselves doing it.

We seem to see so clearly "out there," while "in
here" is a muddle. Relax, it's all part of this addictive
disease process. It's called denial. Breaking through
the denial about what is really going on in our lives is
the first step in recovery.

MAYBE *what we notice "out there" is what we need to
see "in here." I'll check that out.*

HAPPINESS/DEPRESSION

When a small child . . . I thought that success spelled happiness. I was wrong, happiness is like a butterfly which appears and delights us for one brief moment, but soon flits away.

—Anna Pavlova

There is no difference between happiness and depression. They both have the same process. It is just the content that is not the same. Both will come and go. The major difference between them is what we *do* with them.

We are always seeking happiness. When we see it coming we say, "Ah, come here, I see you. Stay with me always." Happiness laughs and says, "Oh, she's seen me, I can leave now." And it does.

With depression, we see it coming, and we say: "Go away, I don't want you. Not me." And depression sighs and says, "Here we go again, I'm going to have to get bigger and bigger for her to hear me and learn what I have to teach." So it taps us on the shoulder and says, "Over here, over here!" until it gets our attention. Then it leaves.

Both happiness and depression have something to teach us. Both will come and go. Both will return. It is our response and openness to learn from both that makes the difference.

———————

MY HAPPINESS *is a gift. My depression is a gift. Both are like butterflies in my life.*

August 1

JOYFULNESS

*Not all songs are religious, but there is scarcely a task,
light or grave, scarcely an event, great or small, but it
has its fitting song.*

—Natalie Curtis

How long has it been since we let ourselves savor the
pure joy of listening to music? I am not talking about
the songs on the radio that we crowd in as we speed
along the freeway. I am talking about the sheer joy of
bathing ourselves in the music we like the most.

Likewise, how long has it been since we have let
ourselves hear the song of the task we are doing?
When we do too much, we lose our joy in the doing
and see only the labor and the deadlines. Even when
we do not see the song in our work, it is still there.
We have but to listen.

————————————————

TODAY *I have the opportunity to open myself joyfully
to the music around me.*

HOLIDAYS/VACATIONS

*Travel not only stirs the blood. . . . It also gives strength
to the spirit.*

—Florence Prag Kahn

Part of the destructiveness of being women who do
too much is that we don't take the time for those
things that "stir the blood" and "give strength to the
spirit." We simply do not take time for vacations and
trips with those we love. And even when we do, we
frequently do them like we do the rest of our life—
rushing, pressured, and frantic.

Vacations mean a change of pace, a gentleness with
ourselves, a time of rest and renewal, and a time to
stretch ourselves and encounter new people, new
lands, new ways, and new options. The very newness
opens the possibility of expanding our spirits and
flushing out the stagnant particles in our blood.

———————————

WE OWE *it to ourselves and those around us to take
vacations.*

FREEDOM

Would you sell the colors of your sunset and the
  fragrance
Of your flowers, and the passionate wonder of
  your forest
For a creed that will not let you dance?
                    —Helene Johnson

Would you? Have you? What kind of creed have we accepted that tells us that we are of no value unless we are working ourselves to death? What kind of creed have we adhered to that tells us that *doing* is superior to *being*? What belief have we accepted that suggests that, if we are not rushing and hurrying, we have no meaning?

We don't have time for sunsets, fragrances of flowers, or the "passionate wonder of our forests." We don't even see sunsets, flowers, or forests. Do they still exist?

Dancing surely must be for pagans who don't have to make money. We used to dance before we became so important.

WHEN *a creed is not articulated as a creed and is assumed to be reality, we don't have much freedom of choice.*

August 4

WORK/TRUTH

I was brought up to believe that the only thing worth doing was to add to the sum of accurate information in the world.

—Margaret Mead

We live in a time of intense information exchange so rapid that it boggles the mind. We are constantly bombarded with news items, new scientific information, new ideas, and new possibilities. Where do we fit? What is our place in all this?

As women, we often discount our knowledge and try to skew our information or our perceptions so that they are acceptable to others. In so doing, we rob the world of our accumulated knowledge. Accurate information is important to the world. Accurate information from a variety of perspectives is *essential*.

I DO *have a place and my information* is *important.*

August 5

AMBITION

Why do you climb philosophical hills? Because they are worth climbing. . . . There are no hills to go down unless you start from the top.
—Margaret Thatcher

One of the marks of an intelligent person is to be able to distinguish what is worth doing and what isn't and to be able to set priorities. The significance of the climb may not be in reaching the top. One can go down a hill from halfway up or from three-quarters of the way up. Or it may be more interesting and intriguing to walk around the hill.

To have the opportunity to explore the philosophical hill, we must step on to it. From then on it is in the process of the walking and noticing the rocks, plants, and strangers along the way that wisdom comes.

GETTING *to the top isn't bad, and it is probably best done as an afterthought.*

August 6

GRATITUDE

Big Blue Mountain Spirit,
The home made of blue clouds . . .
I am grateful for that mode of goodness there.
                                        —Apache chant

It is impossible to come into contact with Native American spirituality and not be struck with the immensity of the gratitude expressed. Theirs is a gentle, quiet, flowing form of gratitude that runs as deep as the still lakes and soars as high as the peaked mountains. The Native American form of gratitude is peaceful. This peacefulness permeates all their legends and stories.

Sometimes we feel that if everything isn't perfect, we cannot be grateful for anything. We easily fall into all-or-nothing thinking. When we do, we miss the sunrise and the other forms of goodness that surround us.

I AM GRATEFUL. *Perhaps that is enough. I am grateful.*

August 7

GROWTH

Character building begins in our infancy and continues until death.
—Eleanor Roosevelt

Somehow, we always have the secret hope that we can get ourselves together, work out all our issues, discover all our talents, accept our life's work, and then relax and get on with it.

What a shock it is when we finally recognize that "character building" and growth are life-long processes and continue throughout our lives. Just when we think we are clear about the direction of our lives, and we settle into that security (stagnation), something shakes our complacency. How much easier it is to recognize in the first place that life is a process and to open ourselves to the cycles of growth in ourselves.

TO GROW *and develop is the normal state for the human organism. . . . I am a human organism. It would be logical, therefore, to assume that growth and development are normal for me.*

August 8

ENTHUSIASM

Whenever I have to choose between two evils, I always like to try the one I haven't tried before.
—Mae West

Mae West was a rough-and-tumble lady (no pun intended) who always exhibited enthusiasm and lust for life. Whenever we see one of her movies or an interview with her, we are always impressed with her brash vitality. She is a good role model in some ways.

We don't have to be brash and we can learn something about our enthusiasm. Enthusiasm is not rounded. It has pointed corners and it is sometimes irritating to those who don't share it. Many of us have tried to curb our enthusiasm so as not to be offensive. We may even have equated getting rid of it with maturity. What a waste! Another piece of ourselves whacked off.

———————

MY ENTHUSIASM *and my aliveness are intimately connected. And it's just fine for me to have both of them.*

BEING PRESENT TO THE MOMENT

Dying is a wild night and a new road.
                                        —Emily Dickinson

Emily Dickinson was present to the process of her dying when she said these words. She seemed to be fully with herself and, at the same time, open to what would come. When we think of our own death, most of us hope that we can be open to the moment.

For most addicts, the idea of dying and the experience of slowly killing ourselves through overwork is something with which we are comfortable. It is the living of our lives at each moment that terrifies us and that we seek to avoid.

Luckily, we can get through this terror and come to know that we have all the caring support we need to live our lives.

THIS *is my moment. I will live each moment. Then death will be a culmination, not an end.*

GOALS

To have realized your dream makes you feel lost.
                                    —Oriana Fallaci

Several years ago one of my friends called me in a panic. "Anne," she said, "you have to do something immediately! There are some women really hurting out there and nobody knows!"

She had been interviewing women who had been in top executive positions for seven to ten years. She said it was as if they had made the team, and every day they got suited up, got on the bus, and went to the game, but . . . they never got off the bench. At first they were hopeful, but after a few years they had become resigned to the reality that they would never quite belong.

She said that she found more alcoholism, clinical depression, and anorexia-bulimia in this group of women than she had ever seen.

———————————

IT IS NOT *the realization of our dreams that makes us feel lost. It is what happens to us when our dreams become nightmares.*

BUSYNESS

We are always doing something . . . talking, reading, listening to the radio, planning what next. The mind is kept naggingly busy on some easy, unimportant, external thing all day.

—Brenda Ueland

What lengths we go to keep away from ourselves! We have such an inability to relax. There are always just a few more tasks we can get done. Sometimes it almost seems that we are afraid of what might happen if we let our minds be idle for even a moment. We fill in every crack and crevice with activity. Sometimes, we even try to crowd two or more activities in at once, like making out a list of things that need to be done while we watch the news, or directing the activities of the kids while we are working on a report.

We have become addicted to busyness, and if we are not busy we feel worthless, at a loss, and even frightened.

NOTICING *how busy I keep myself is the first step. Realizing that I am powerless over this busyness is the second. Recognizing that my busyness is adversely affecting my life is next.*

August 12

DEFENSIVENESS

I'm defensive even when what's going on has nothing to do with me. I just know I must be wrong somehow.
                                        —Elizabeth

Being on the defensive is part of this cunning, baffling, powerful, and patient disease. If somebody offers some advice or constructive criticism, we immediately feel we are being attacked and need to defend ourselves. Or we feel we must always apologize when *anything goes wrong.* If it is going wrong, it must be our fault. Sometimes we almost seem to be apologizing for our very existence. It is as if we don't have a right to exist.

Our defensiveness, like our other character defects, will lessen as we progress in our recovery. We have but to follow the Twelve-Step program and do our work.

———————————

REMEMBER, *my defensiveness is not who I am, it is what I do when I am operating out of my addictive disease. It is a red flag for me.*

CONTROL

People that keep stiff upper lips find that it's damn hard to smile.

—Judith Guest

We women who do too much sure do enjoy our illusion of control. In fact, it is one of our favorite illusions. Whatever it is, we can just "guts it through." We cannot afford to relax, because we might lose our tenuous hold on the reins.

We try to control everything. We believe that we can trick our bodies into more work and prevent burnout by participating in the appropriate stress management seminars and exercising regularly. We eat the right foods so we can continue to overwork our bodies. We do all the right things to "keep our lives under control." And then we read the statistics that say that death by heart attack is rising for professional women and that the age level is dropping. Surely, if we just do enough we can control . . . our bodies, our lives, and the lives of others.

―――――――――――

NO WONDER *we don't smile much!*

EXPECTATION/SUCCESS

*My expectations—which I extended whenever I came
close to accomplishing my goals—made it impossible
ever to feel satisfied with my success.*
                                        —Ellen Sue Stern

A lot is never enough for women who do too much.
Whenever it looks like we may have the experience of
successfully completing a project, we add on other
contingencies and set up the possibility of doing even
more than we originally had thought possible.

Sometimes we even make tasks more complicated
than they need be so we can keep busy. We feel safer
when we are working. We get panicked with slack
time. We feel it is almost impossible to let ourselves
savor our successes. And, if we would be truthful, we
have many of them.

———————————

IT'S ALL RIGHT *to have successes. It's even all right
to be successful.*

BUSYNESS

I'm a workaholic. If I'm not working I exercise. If I'm not exercising, I eat. I don't ever stop from morning to night.

—Terry

Some of us have modeled our lives after the roadrunner cartoon character: jump out of bed—beep, beep. Throw in a load of laundry so it can wash while we do our exercises and shower—beep, beep. Nine minutes for make-up and hair—beep, beep. Seven minutes for starting the coffee, getting dressed, and popping in the toast. Five minutes for eating breakfast and making out a list of things that must be done today—beep, beep. Throw laundry into the dryer, grab coat, purse, and briefcase, and burst through the front door—beep, beep.

By the time we have finished our morning routine, most people would be exhausted, and we have just begun—beep . . . beep . . .

PERHAPS *it is important to remember that I was not created to be a roadrunner, even if we have some features in common.*

ASKING FOR HELP/REALITY

However, one cannot put a quart in a pint cup.
                    —Charlotte Perkins Gilman

There is a Zen story about a college professor who came to a Zen master seeking knowledge. The old Zen master looked over the professor carefully and then asked a student to go fetch her a pot of tea and two cups. She then placed a cup in front of the professor and began to pour. The tea filled the cup and spilled out over the table. Seeing this, the professor shouted, "Stop, can't you see the cup is full? It can hold no more!" The old Zen master smiled and said, "And so it is with you. Your mind, too, is full of too many things. Only when you empty it will there be room for more knowledge to come in."

Asking for help is a way of "emptying" our lives. Stopping and seeing that our lives have become too full may well be the beginning of a process that can empty us and make way for new ways of being.

MY CUP *runneth over may in some contexts be a declaration of disaster. Emptying is fully as important as filling.*

AWE

But what will never, never change is the wonder, the indescribable wonder to me of seeing Earth lying in space as in the hollow of God's hand.
                                        —Zenna Henderson

Awe is a feeling that is rare in our busy lives. Awe means stopping and noticing. Awe is, at least momentarily, letting ourselves remember and experience the vastness of the universe or the amazingly intricate design in the petal of a tiny flower.

One of my friends from Germany came bearing gifts when she visited. The most intriguing was a tiny one-inch-square magnifying glass which unfolded such that the distance between the end of the stand and the magnifying glass was a little over an inch, exactly the distance needed to see clearly the tiniest veins in a leaf, the detail on the back of a bug, or the center of a minute flower. This little device opened up an entire universe to my awareness. What she had really given me was a gift of awe.

LIFE *without awe is like food without herbs or spices. I have only to look around me to remember the feeling of awe.*

LONELINESS

The thing that makes you exceptional if you are at all, is inevitably that which must also make you lonely.
—Lorraine Hansberry

We are so afraid of experiencing our loneliness that we keep ourselves overscheduled and constantly busy. Often it is our fear of loneliness that is much more disabling than loneliness itself. We are so afraid of being alone that we make sure we never are.

Yet experiencing our loneliness and going through it is often the door to those parts of our being which are creative and exceptional.

I was recently given a tee shirt from a woman's bookstore that said, "Flaunt your uniqueness." We fear that if we really let people see who we are, we will be isolated. We fail to see that isolation and loneliness are different from being alone.

———————

I WILL *remember that to be lonely is not to die. My loneliness is mine. I may even learn something from it.*

EXHAUSTION

*I use food and caffeine addictions to keep going when
I am too tired to get the job done or meet deadlines.*
                                    —Anonymous

No one has just one addiction. Addictions come in clusters. Frequently we use one addiction to support another or to mask another. When our body is just too
tired from working too much we use chemicals or
food to keep us going. When we are too buzzed up to
let down after we have met a deadline, we use food,
alcohol, or prescription drugs to slow us down.

We have even used positive activities to support
our busyness and our workaholism. Exercise is good
for us. Unfortunately, when we do it in a frantic way
or when we use it to make our bodies healthier so we
can work more, something good has become part of
the problem. We can use anything to "protect our
supply" and allow us to stay in our addiction.

———————————

IT IS NOT what *I do, it is the* way *I do it, that will
get me in the end.*

SADNESS/MOVING ON

If ever I had a good mind, it has been lost in the shuffle. I seem to have stagnated, and I am aware that I am not using any capacity I have to the fullest.
                                                    —Anonymous

Resignation . . . despair . . . a sadness in lost possibilities. It's time to take stock and realign our priorities. We seem to have wandered off our path. Perhaps we have even forgotten what our path was.

Maybe it is time to feel the grief of lost opportunities and stagnating minds. Life often teaches us through our wrong turns and missed possibilities. This feeling of sadness may well be the door to a new beginning. But we will never go through the new door if we do not let ourselves go through the grief and sadness.

As we let ourselves feel our grief and pain, we will truly have the opportunity to step onto a new path and to explore our lives.

———————————————

MY GRIEF *and pain are mine. I have earned them. They are part of me. Only in feeling them do I open myself to the lessons they can teach.*

DUTY

Duty should be a byproduct.

—Brenda Ueland

Addictive thinking usually results in putting the cart before the donkey. One of the fascinating skills of addiction is that it allows us to take something relatively neutral or even good and twist it ever so slightly, so that it becomes horrendous.

There's nothing wrong with duty. We just should not let duty override our clear feelings and intuitions. Duty cannot come before our own internal clarity. When it does, it is a tyrant. Duty needs to follow our clarity, just as doing things for our loved ones needs to be an expression of love, rather than ritualized behavior. Duty needs to be a by-product of who we truly are, and what we value, and what is important to us.

———————————

RITUALIZED *duty is a sham!*

WONDER

If a child is to keep alive his inborn sense of wonder without any such gift from the fairies, he needs the companionship of at least one adult who can share it, rediscovering with him the joy, excitement, and mystery of the world we live in.

—Rachel Carson

How fortunate if we get to be that adult who has the opportunity to be a companion to a child and support that child's sense of wonder! We are lucky because that child can offer us the opportunity to rekindle our own awareness that wonder continues to dwell in us. That child can remind us that we still have the capacity to look at cloud formations with new eyes and to giggle in excitement with a new discovery. How long has it been since we really had a belly laugh, especially at ourselves? How long has it been since we saw a rainbow in a drop of rain? How long since we studied the progress of a red and black ladybug on our hand?

I WONDER *where our wonder is?*

STRUGGLE

You wear yourself out in the pursuit of wealth or love or freedom, you do everything to gain some right, and once it's gained, you take no pleasure in it.
                                        —Oriana Fallaci

Sometimes we forget what's important. We struggle so long to establish ourselves that we become addicted to the struggle. We begin to think that if we are not struggling we are not alive. In fact, the excitement and intensity of the struggle become our complete focus, so that we forget our original goal.

There is no doubt that we as women have had to struggle individually and as a group. Yet, if we become like those against whom we struggle, we may find that we have lost ourselves in the process.

———————————

SOMETIMES *we have to struggle . . . sometimes not. The issue is not the romance of the struggle; the issue is who we are as we engage in it.*

SECRETS

As awareness increases, the need for personal secrecy almost proportionately decreases.
						—Charlotte Painter

As Isak Dinesen says, "a secret is an ugly thing." In the Twelve-Step program of Alcoholics Anonymous, we often hear the phrase, "you are as sick as the secrets you keep."

Often we fail to recognize the effect that secrets have on our lives. They are like a quiet cancer that eats away at our souls and devours our relationships. When we enter into a contract of secrecy with someone, we give a little piece of ourselves away. If we give away too many pieces of ourselves, we are devoured, very much like the heroine in Margaret Atwood's novel, *Edible Woman*.

An important part of recovery from the addictive process is to give up secret-keeping. It is only when we live our life in the open, accept responsibility for the decisions that we have made, and own our behavior that we begin to know health.

———————————

AS THE FRENCH *say, "Nothing is so burdensome as a secret."*

HAPPINESS/CONTROL

They seemed to come suddenly upon happiness as if they had surprised a butterfly in the winter woods.
—Edith Wharton

Happiness, like most of the other important processes of life, cannot be planned. We often come to believe that if we just had an important job, plenty of money, the right relationship, attractive and intelligent kids, and a lovely home, we would be happy. When we attain these goals and still secretly feel depressed, or not quite fulfilled, we immediately ask ourselves, "What's wrong with me?"

We have done all the things that are supposed to bring us happiness, and we don't feel any better. Where have we gone wrong? We always question ourselves and believe that there is something innately wrong with us. It takes us a long time to stop and question the system that taught us that accumulation and control are the vehicles to happiness.

———————

HAPPINESS *is a gift. It comes like "a butterfly in the winter woods." Let it sit with us a while.*

PARENTING

So learning (making, coming to) rather than accomplishment is the issue in parenthood.
— Polly Berrien Berends

How confused we get about parenting! So often, we are stuck in the amazing belief that it is our responsibility to *teach* our children. We forget that it is equally as important to *learn* from them. Some of our children don't take their responsibility to teach us seriously, but then again parents are notoriously slow learners.

It is difficult for us to learn something when we believe that all teaching should go in one direction. How much we miss in that arrogance.

———————————

PERHAPS *one of the reasons my child chose me as her parent was because there was so much I needed to learn.*

LONELINESS

Because they are cut off from their internal power source, they really feel alone and lost.
—Shakti Gawain

When we think about what is missing from our lives, we may come to the conclusion that *we are!* Oh, of course, we function well. We do the things that need to get done. We are even efficient and imaginative at times, and yet so often we feel like zombies carrying out an old routine in well-worn ruts. We have lost touch with ourselves, and there is nothing lonelier than not being in touch with ourselves.

When we have lost ourselves, no amount of externals will help. Spouses, friends, work—none can supply what is missing when we are cut off from our "internal power source." *We* are missing, and the only way to remedy this problem is to find ourselves again. Finding ourselves takes time. It is hard work *and* it is worth doing.

————————————

I WAS *looking all over for what was missing in my life, and then I discovered I was.*

August 28

HUMOR/RELATIONSHIPS

*When you see what some girls marry, you realize how
they must hate to work for a living.*
                                        —Helen Rowland

What a joke. Some of us thought if we just married
the right man, or found the right partner, we would-
n't have to work. Did we ever consider how much
work it is to be married to someone so we won't have
to work? Did we ever consider how much work it is
not to do *our work?* Did we ever consider that our
work is not work but *our work?*

How tempting it is to sell our souls for what we
think will be the prize! We women have been too
willing to objectify . . . to make ourselves sex objects
and make men (or other women) marriage objects. In
so doing we have lost the possibilities of relationships.
It is not possible to relate to an object.

───────────────

REMEMBER, *one has to* perform *to get the prize.
One has to* be *to relate.*

IMPRESSION MANAGEMENT

Women's virtue is man's greatest invention.
— Cornelia Otis Skinner

How much we distort ourselves in trying to please others. Women have historically been controlled by the demands and expectations of others. We have been so willing to let others define us and so eager to fit that definition that we have lost all track of who we are.

As we come more in contact with ourselves, we realize that many of the definitions of who women "naturally are" are generated to take care of others. For example, it has been an accepted truth of psychology that women are "natural nesters." Yet, in recent times, when women have been getting divorced, it appears that it is the men who quickly find another woman to make a nest for them, while women become the wanderers. So many of our definitions of who we are have been invented for us by others, to please them and meet their needs—and we have desperately tried to fit their images of what is acceptable.

———————

A VIRTUOUS *woman is someone who is herself.*

INTERRUPTIONS

*It is distraction, not meditation, that becomes habitual;
interruption, not continuity; spasmodic, not constant
toil.*

—Tillie Olsen

How we hate interruptions, especially when we are
working on something important. In fact, when we
are working on something important, everything is an
interruption. As Tillie Olsen says, distraction, interruption, and the spasmodic seem to be our lot sometimes.

How difficult it is to mesh the process of our life
and the process of our work. Yet, how sweet it is
when that happens!

One of the reasons that "meditation," "continuity,"
and "constant toil" have not been possible is because
we have not believed that we deserve the time for
ourselves to do our own work. Just as the addict who
is into her self-centeredness is out of touch with herself, the workaholic who is into her workaholism is
out of touch with her work.

———————

WHEN *I trust my process, I trust the process of my
work.*

ALONE TIME

So you see, imagination needs moodling,——long, inef-
ficient, happy idling, dawdling and puttering.
                                    —Brenda Ueland

What wonderful words: moodling, dawdling, and
puttering! I have a friend who says that she likes to
"frither." The word sounds just like what it is: putz-
ing—really doing nothing.

I used to have a big dog named Bubber who was
one of my most important teachers. He used to sit
out on our deck up in the mountains and just look. It
was difficult for me to imagine what he was looking at
all the time, so one day I just went out and sat beside
him and "looked." I sat with him for a long time and
experienced just sitting and just looking. I learned to
take time just to sit and look. One sees so much when
one just sits and *looks*. Doing nothing else . . . just
looking.

Bubber has since died, and his great wisdom in having taught me to sit and look lives on.

———————————

NOT ALL *of us can have Bubbers,* and *all of us can*
develop the skill to sit and look.

HONESTY

I give myself sometimes admirable advice, but I am in-capable of taking it.
—Mary Wortley Montagu

How refreshing when we can be honest, even humor-ously honest, about ourselves! Often we are so busy protecting ourselves that we don't dare risk letting others know that we aren't perfect. Of course, usually we are the only ones fooled by our masquerades, but we make ourselves believe that others are fooled, too.

When we can be honest with ourselves, we usually know very clearly what we need and what is destruc-tive to us. The trick is, can we listen to ourselves? Are we capable of following our own good advice? Can we let ourselves see our foibles and laugh about them? After all, no one knows us as well as we know our-selves. So, naturally, we are the persons who are most capable of seeing ourselves clearly. Are we courageous enough to let ourselves see ourselves and be honest about what we see?

———————

ADVICE *is difficult, even when it comes from our-selves. Even if we can't put our advice into action, we don't need to beat ourselves up about it.*

JOYFULNESS/CONTROL

In search of my mother's garden I found my own.
                                          —Alice Walker

One of the greatest joys in life is to be in search of one thing and to discover another.

Before we started our recovery, we were so controlling that surprises struck terror in our heart even when they were wonderful. We just didn't want anything coming at us that wasn't planned, structured, and under control. We now realize that trying to control everything has been one of the ways that we have robbed ourselves of the joy of living.

No wonder life has seemed dull at times—we have made it that way. It's not that the potential for joy wasn't there. We just were too busy and controlling to notice it.

——————————

THE PURE *joyfulness of the unexpected can be a source of wonder to me.*

IN TOUCH WITH A POWER
GREATER THAN ONESELF

Those who lose dreaming are lost.
                —Australian Aboriginal proverb

If we are to have any hope of being in touch with the process of the universe or with a power greater than ourselves, we must learn to move beyond our rational, logical minds and to let ourselves "dream."

That does not mean that there is anything wrong with our rational, logical minds, but we can have trouble connecting with a force greater than ourselves when we *lead* with our rational minds.

There are so many things in this universe that affect us and with which we are connected. Sometimes the only way we can be aware of that connection is to let ourselves dream beyond our knowing. We have so much to learn from everything around us, if we just open ourselves to that which may be.

———————

I ADMIT *I don't know it all yet. Learning comes in many forms.*

September 4

LEARNING

Patterns of the past echo in the present and resound through the future.
                                            —Dhyani Ywahoo

We are a process, and the key to living that process is learning. Mistakes are not proof that we are bad; they are doors for learning and moving on. It is often said of addicts that they don't learn from their past because they have no memory. If we have no past, we have no present and we have no future.

Everything in our lives is an opportunity for learning. Often, our most painful experiences open doors that must be opened before we can take our next steps. That doesn't mean that we don't sometimes have to walk over what seem like beds of hot coals to reach the door. Yet once we reach the other side the learning is there.

Kurt Vonnegut talks about "wrang-wrangs" in our lives, great teachers who are placed in our path. The lessons they teach us are vastly important, and they are taught through struggle, pain, trial, and tribulation. Still, they are important teachers.

———————————

THE NEXT TIME *a "wrang-wrang" drops into my life, I have the option of recognizing that person as a teacher.*

September 5

AWARENESS/CONTROL

Discoveries have reverberations. A new idea about one-self or some aspect of one's relations to others unsettles all one's other ideas, even the superficially related ones. No matter how slightly, it shifts one's entire orientation. And somewhere along the line of consequences, it changes one's behavior.

—Patricia McLaughlin

How amazing we human beings are! One little change in any aspect of our life affects so many other facets of our being in as yet unimagined or undreamed of ways that we never really quite know where anything will lead. We say no to something at work that for many months we have wanted to say no to and instead of the backlash we expected, we experience some subtle indication of respect. We certainly respect ourselves more.

We break our necks to earn respect and admiration, only to discover that we really have no control over how others perceive us. Our letting go of our illusion of control in even the smallest way reverberates throughout our lives.

———————

I KNOW *that gradually, ever so gradually, I am growing and changing. My life is much more like a mobile than a ladder. Each new discovery affects every aspect of my being.*

September 6

COMPETITIVENESS/OPTIONS

The only way we got any attention from our father was if we made straight A's, he would give us three dollars. You can bet I worked my tail off. It wasn't the money either. Sooo, the seeds of my workaholism were planted early.

—Mary

How subtly we are given the message that we are what we produce! Acceptance and approval were very important to us as children, and we could get them by "working our tails off." Unfortunately, no matter what we did or how well we did it, it never seemed to be enough. At least, it did not really take care of that longing inside that is sometimes so intense it hurts.

Getting rewards and recognition can take away the growing internal pain momentarily, but it always comes back. We can get our three-dollar award as children, or we can get impressive salaries and positions as adults, and somehow the emptiness inside just goes underground. It does not disappear.

The seeds of our workaholism and busyness were indeed sown early. We must, however, remember that anything that has been learned can be unlearned. We were not created to work ourselves to death. We have *learned* to work ourselves to death.

I HAVE OPTIONS *for my life, and one option is to see options.*

DEMANDING TOO MUCH
OF ONESELF

I believe that IQ's change, and mine dropped consider-
ably. I'm no longer very competent in any area. My
children all turned out well not due to me, but rather
to a strict father who allowed no nonsense.

—Anonymous

What has happened to this woman? Where did she go?
As we read what she says about herself, we have the
feeling that she is disappearing before our very eyes.
Many of us have had the experience of being devoured by our families, our houses, our jobs, and our
lives. I once knew a woman who used to keep looking
back for footprints on the sidewalk, because she had
the strange feeling that her soul was seeping out
through the soles of her feet and she would see the evidence on the sidewalk.

I can remember feeling as if I did not exist as a
separate person when I used to work at the kitchen
counter and my children would stand on my feet to
make themselves just a little higher. I also felt myself
disappearing when, as toddlers, they wanted to get
from one end of the couch to the other and they just
walked over me as if I were not there. Life can, at
times, invite us to disappear.

We feel ourselves disappearing. Yet, how arrogant it
is for the woman quoted above to accept that her children turned out well and to believe that she had nothing to do with it! What a dedication to self abnegation!

TODAY, *I will be willing to look at the possibility*
that my self-battering is an arrogant and self-centered
activity that is not useful to me or anyone else.

September 8

AMBITION

Sometimes you wonder how you got on this mountain.
But sometimes you wonder, "How will I get off?"
                                        —Joan Manley

Ambition has been important to many of us. When we were little girls, we realized that it was important that we work hard and become somebody. We wanted to get ahead, and we were willing to go to any lengths to be competent and important. In the last few years women have had many more options for our lives, and we wanted to take advantage of these opportunities.

When did things change? When did we cross over the line from having ambition, which was good, to being had by our ambition, which is killing us?

Often, with addictions, the very skills which kept us alive when we were younger (like dishonesty, control, and manipulation) are now lethal and are draining the life from us. This may be true about our ambition. If it now is running our lives, it may be time to take another look.

———————————

WHAT WAS GOOD *for us at one stage of our lives may be lethal now. We need to take stock and see where we are with our lives.*

September 9

WISDOM

Women have always been the guardians of wisdom and humanity which makes them natural, but usually secret, rulers. The time has come for them to rule openly, but together with and not against men.
                                              —Charlotte Wolf

It is time to listen—to listen to myself and to listen to the ancient wisdom that is all around me.

Women are such masters of practical wisdom and we live in a world that is dying for lack of practicality. What good is the best invention in the world if it doesn't *work?* What good are the best ideas in the world if we cannot use them?

If we are indeed the guardians of wisdom, it behooves us to share that wisdom.

———————————

AS MERIDEL LE SUEUR *says,* "*The rites of ancient ripening / Make my flesh plume.*"

STARTING OVER

The two important things I did learn were that you are as powerful and strong as you allow yourself to be, and that the most difficult part of any endeavor is taking the first step, making the first decision.
—Robyn Davidson

These words were written by a woman who learned to handle camels and traveled alone with them across the Australian Outback. Somehow the intensity of the circumstances under which she gathered these learnings makes them even more profound. What if each of us believed that we are "as powerful and strong" as we allow ourselves to be? What if we quit trying to be accepted by everyone and gave up trying not to alienate anyone and just let ourselves be as strong and powerful as we are? Nothing extraordinary, mind you, just as wonderfully powerful as we naturally are.

And, what if we let ourself take that first step toward what we really want? Nothing big . . . no fanfares . . . just do it!

REMEMBER *today really is the first day of the rest of my life.*

SERENITY

The silence of a shut park does not sound like country silence; it is tense and confined.
—Elizabeth Bowen

When we are not really dealing with our disease of doing too much, we are often silent and not serene. We have only shut up for awhile and are still "tense and confined," like a city park shut off from activity.

Serenity is more like having a "country silence" within. Serenity is an acceptance of who we are and a *being* of who we are. Serenity is an awareness of our place in the universe and a oneness with all things.

Serenity is active. It is a gentle and firm participation with trust. Serenity is the relaxation of our cells into who we are and a quiet celebration of that relaxation.

———————————

LONGINGLY, *way back somewhere, I remember what it is like to have a "country silence" within. I can be grateful for that sense of knowing.*

REACHING OUR LIMITS

I have had enough.

—Golda Meir

What beautiful words, and how rarely are they spoken by women who do too much. Part of our craziness is not recognizing that we have limits and not knowing when we reach them. In fact, many of us may see having limits as an indicator of inadequacy. We cannot forgive ourselves for not being able to carry on when we are exhausted or for not being able to keep going regardless of the circumstances.

Recognizing that we are approaching our limits and accepting those limits may be the beginning of recovery.

———————

EVERY *human being has limits, and I am a human being.*

LIVING LIFE FULLY

She wants to live for once. But doesn't know quite what that means. Wonders if she has ever done it. If she ever will.

—Alice Walker

Most of us would like to live life fully. Yet when it comes to putting those words into practice, we are not quite sure how. We wonder if we know what living life fully really means, or if we have ever known.

Our temptation is to rush out and stock up on "how to" books. If we can just find the right book, we will know what to do. We have read enough so that we are pretty good at following directions. Or we start going to lectures and workshops. We try meditation, drumming, chanting, special diets, special exercises, and special therapies. Always looking outside ourselves for the formula and answers.

At some point we realize that in spite of how good all these approaches are, we have to come back to the realization that only *we* know how to live *our lives* fully. We can accept guideposts, and ultimately, living our lives is up to us.

———————

EVEN IF *we have never done it, the knowledge of how to live our lives fully lies deep within us.*

September 14

FEELING OVERWHELMED

Feeling overwhelmed isn't surprising. Being surprised about it is.

Anne Wilson Schaef

Is it any wonder we often feel overwhelmed? Just the bills for all the "necessities" of life seem more than we can handle sometimes. And then there are federal income taxes, state taxes, changing deductions, investments, sales, best buys, 10,000-mile checkups on our cars, teeth cleaning, pap smears, travel arrangements, and planning family vacations, if we dare to take one.

Recent estimates on the rate of information processing tell us that every few minutes we process more information than was processed in a lifetime by those living in the Middle Ages.

Feeling overwhelmed feels like a normal reaction.

———————————

SOMETIMES *it helps to know that I just can't do it all. One step at a time is all that's possible—even when those steps are taken on the run.*

FEELINGS

Sorrow is tranquility remembered in emotion.
—Dorothy Parker

How lovely! All feelings are equally as lovely.

We have done ourselves such a disservice by talking about "negative" and "positive" feelings. Feelings are just feelings, and like every other aspect of our being are gifts from which we can learn.

Sorrow and grieving are feelings that we try to avoid. They take time and are not easy. Yet we make them worse by avoiding them. We feel sad when some promotion doesn't come through. We feel sorrow when we lose those we love. How beautiful to think of it as "tranquility remembered in emotion."

Grief is real, and it is human. We grieve our losses, whatever they are. Grief is an unfolding process that has many levels. It is important for us to accept our passage through the levels of grief. It is even normal to feel grief when we finish an interesting project, or when our company or family restructures.

IT IS FIGHTING *our feelings that causes our suffering, not our feelings.*

BEING OBSESSED

*I feel when people say "bigger and better" they should
say "bigger and badder."*
                              —Marie Elizabeth Kane
                                 (13 years old)

Women who do too much have embraced the cultural expectation of more, more, more. We want
more money, more power, more recognition, more
acceptance, more. . . . We become obsessed with getting whatever it is we feel that we must get. As our
addictions progress, our values regress.

It is easy to see how an alcoholic or drug addict will
do anything for a fix. But workaholics and careaholics
can become just as deadly when their supply is threatened. The cornerstone of any addictive behavior is a
loss of touch with our own morality and spirituality.
We become "spiritually bankrupt." We get "bigger and
badder."

———————

IT IS *a relief to know that recovery from any addiction is guaranteed if I just do the work I need to do. I
really don't want to be one of the bad guys.*

GIFTS/WORRYING

I think these difficult times have helped me to under-
stand better than before how infinitely rich and beau-
tiful life is in every way and that so many things that
one goes around worrying about are of no importance
whatsoever.

—Isak Dinesen

It's not that we need to seek pain and suffering to glean the rich learnings of life. When they happen, however, we learn so much more if we can see these situations as rich opportunities for learning. We spend so much time worrying, and worrying is nothing more than an attempt at remote control. Often what we worry about never comes to pass. Unfortunately, we may be so preoccupied with worry that we miss the gifts our life is presenting to us at the moment.

When will we realize that the unfolding process of our lives is so much richer and varied than we ever could have planned? The unplanned and uncontrollable gifts we receive add color to the tapestry of living.

———————

I NEVER KNOW *in advance what will be an impor-*
tant gift for me. Hence it behooves me to be open to
possibilities.

GUILT

I even feel guilty about feeling guilty.

—Nicole

Women are the first in line to stand up for a good cause. We can mobilize an army of volunteers to save a faltering school system, a crumbling church, or a sagging corporation. We are willing and able to put our weight behind any cause that is politically correct. We genuinely care about the homeless, the starving, the brutalized, and the forgotten, and we do a great deal of good. Who knows how much of our causes are motivated by guilt? Only we can know that, as we look inside.

The one cause that we have difficulty supporting is that of women. We are covered with guilt if we take a stand on our own behalf. We believe we should always be putting our energies "out there" for those who need it more. Women are notorious for not recognizing and standing up for our own needs and, on those rare occasions when we do, we are quickly immobilized when anyone calls us selfish.

GIVING OUT *of guilt is like sharing an apple full of worms. We have to take care of ourselves before we can clearly and cleanly give to others.*

BEING PRESENT TO THE MOMENT

What they took for inattentiveness was a miracle of concentration.

—Toni Morrison

Have you ever watched a cat stalk a bird? Every muscle, every tendon, every heartbeat is focused on the prey.

Have you ever watched a cat stretch after a nap? Every muscle, every tendon, every heartbeat is totally involved in the stretch.

Sometimes when we are totally concentrating on a task we may seem rude and inattentive. Yet we are wholly present. We are present to our moment of focus.

These moments of complete focus are magical moments and frequently are times when we experience the oneness with our Higher Power and the process of the universe. We are totally within ourselves, and we are totally beyond ourselves.

———————

I REJOICE *for the moments of total oneness. I am truly myself when within and beyond myself.*

CONTROL/COURAGE

Even cowards can endure hardship; only the brave can endure suspense.
                                        —Mignon McLaughlin

Before we started our recovery program, we never thought that we could tolerate the suspense of living. We believed that if we could just control everything— how people see us, how our children turn out, how a client progresses—then we would be safe.

As we have begun to let go of our illusion of control, we find that life is indeed scary sometimes (of course it was before, too, but we just didn't let ourselves feel our feelings). We also find that it holds the potential of undreamed-of surprises and suspenseful moments that we handle well and from which we grow.

————————————

I ALWAYS *thought it true courage to suffer. Now I see that being alive is a special kind of bravery.*

CLARITY

Women know a lot of things they don't read in the newspapers. It's pretty funny sometimes, how women know a lot of things and nobody can figure out how they know them.

—Meridel Le Sueur

What a struggle it has been for us to repress our knowing for all these years . . . for all these centuries. Our addiction to doing too much enables us to ignore our own wisdom, so that we fit more easily into an addictive society.

How often have we kept our mouths shut at board meetings and staff meetings because sharing our knowledge would arouse a great hue and cry, or be completely ignored?

We have tried so hard to fit into a society that we did not create and to become acceptable to that society that we have become the amazing shrinking women. Yet, we know and we know we know.

THE WORLD *needs our knowledge and our wisdom. Our companies need our clarity. Our families need our clarity. We need our clarity.*

CONFUSION

I seem to have an awful lot of people inside me.
——Dame Edith Evans

Frequently it is the people that we carry around inside us who encourage our workaholism, our busyness and our careaholism.

We have little voices in our minds that tell us, "You are expendable. Employers can get rid of people who are not high producers. You are what you do. If you aren't doing something, you are nothing. No one will ever want you just for who you are. You have to make yourself indispensable, and then you can feel secure. You aren't intelligent *enough*. You're *too* intelligent." Voices, voices, voices.

No wonder we often feel confused. We have a chorus on twenty-four-hour duty.

———————————

GROWING UP *and claiming our own lives is partially a process of listening to our own voices and distinguishing them from the crowd inside us, especially when the internal committee is a group of addicts.*

CONFUSION/DOING IT ALL

Being a "good mother" does not call for the same qualities as being a "good" housewife, and the pressure to be both at the same time may be an insupportable burden.

—Ann Oakley

Trying to be all things to all people is characteristic of women who do too much. We accept a number of roles, many of which are contradictory in their demands on us and the skills they require. We find that the skills we need to communicate in the world of business are disastrous when used with our children. And the skills we need to be good mothers are not valued in the workplace. Is it any wonder that we feel confused?

Thank goodness recovery gives us a model for operating out of ourselves and not trying to fit ourselves into roles and become those roles.

WHEN I BRING MYSELF *to a situation, that is the best I have to offer.*

BALANCE

There is a time for work. And a time for love. That leaves no other time.

—Coco Chanel

Well, at least Coco Chanel recognized that one has to do something besides work! How many of us have ruled out love and living from our lives and seen them as expendable? Even if we are married, we act as if love is a luxury that we can ill afford. Our disease of doing too much has isolated us more and more from ourselves and others.

Just as nature needs balance, people need balance. We need time to be whole persons, and this means balance. We are constantly being drained. Therefore, we need to be fed, and we need time to digest the nourishment. Work and love are better than just work alone and . . . there is more.

————————————

A HUMAN BEING *is multidimensional. A human doing may be more like a drawn line than a faceted gem.*

September 25

CONFUSED THINKING

Every time you don't follow your inner guidance, you feel a loss of energy, loss of power, a sense of spiritual deadness.

—Shakti Gawain

Sometimes we just think too much. We have a problem to solve, and we believe that if we just can figure it out we will be all right. The more we figure, the more confused we become, until we have ourselves in a complete muddle. Then we use this occasion to beat ourselves up for being so dumb and stupid that we can't figure out the solution—and the downward spiral continues. We are in our disease of addiction. We are operating out of the addictive process. We are indeed experiencing a loss of energy, a loss of power, a sense of spiritual deadness.

———

STOP!! *It's time to wait with our "inner guidance." It's always there. We have just covered it over with the compacted concentration of mental masturbation.*

AMENDS/PARENTING/CONTROL/
SELF-CENTEREDNESS
STEPS EIGHT AND NINE

I treated my children like projects, efficiently managing and orchestrating their lives, often at the expense of their feelings.

—Ellen Sue Stern

As we begin to look at the effects of trying to control everything and "efficiently manage and orchestrate" our lives and the lives of those around us, we realize that, just like the alcoholic, our disease has seriously damaged those we love the most. They are victims of our disease as much as the family of an alcoholic or a drug addict is a victim of the disease.

We begin to see that in our confused, diseased way of thinking, what we thought was good for our children and those we love was really a self-centered way of trying to stay in control.

Seeing what we have been doing is the first step toward recovery. We need to admit what we, perhaps unwittingly, have done to others, and, where possible, without harming them, make amends.

————————

AS I LOOK BACK *on my enmeshment in my work, I am not always proud of what I have done. I hope, however, that I have another chance with those I love.*

HONORING SELF/PANIC/
CHOICES/SUPPORT

*The place where I work is supposed to be a place that
heals people, and it violates the people who work there.*
—Rosie

We have been hearing more and more about unhealthy
buildings and their effect upon our lives. However, as
many of us begin our recovery and start to take better
care of ourselves, we discover that our workplaces not
only do not support our quest to become healthier,
they actively interfere with it.

We find ourselves feeling frightened and overwhelmed. Are we going to have to give up our jobs to
be healthy? Are we going to have to give up our journey into health in order to maintain our jobs? Neither
option is too attractive.

Luckily, we do not have to make either of these
choices today. We *do* need to get support for our journey toward health, however. Hopefully, there are possibilities for this support within and outside of the
work setting. Support is crucial for becoming more
whole.

———————————

I WILL *look around and open myself to as yet undis-
covered sources of support wherever they are available.*

INDISPENSABLE

But my family needs me.
—Anonymous housewife

There is nothing as secure as being needed . . . or is there?

There is nothing as draining as being needed. We have often made ourselves indispensable at work and at home so that we would feel secure and wanted. Down deep it was inconceivable that people in our lives could love us for who we are. Even if they might, could we afford to take the risk and let their love come to us?

Of course our children need us, but often much less than we wish. Unfortunately, trying to make ourselves indispensable is not relegated to the home and women who work in the home. Often we equate being indispensable with being secure. In fact, we confuse the two.

———————————

WHEN I AM *trying to make myself indispensable, I know that I need to look inside to see what I am feeling.*

September 29

BUSYNESS/FRIENDSHIP

What a new idea! I had this friend who came to visit and it dawned on me . . . I didn't have to do anything.
                                                    —Mary

We busyaholics cannot even imagine the possibility of not having to *do* something. When a friend comes to visit, that gives us the opportunity to indulge in our disease—rushing around, getting things in order, arranging, and preparing so they will feel welcome and have a good time.

We are so busy *before* they arrive that we are exhausted *when* they arrive. Or we keep ourselves so busy making them comfortable that we do not get to sit and be with them.

Somewhere in our busy little beings it is inconceivable that they can care for themselves and they just wanted to be with *us*.

———————————

TODAY *I have the possibility to be open to the possibility that someone who reaches out just wants to be with* me.

FEAR/WORK

Know that it is good to work. Work with love and think
of liking it when you do it. It is easy and interesting. It
is a privilege. There is nothing hard about it but your
anxious vanity and fear of failure.

—Brenda Ueland

Our work and the ability to do our work are gifts we
have. Doing our work is so simple. We just do it. Our
work is not difficult, confounding, or complicated. We
make it that way sometimes. When we are able to
focus on our work and just get down to it and do it
one step at a time, it gets done and it usually gets done
well. When we overwhelm ourselves by seeing only
the totality of it looming before us and do not break it
down into its smaller components, we begin to feel
inadequate and incapable of completing the task. We
then procrastinate as our anxiety and fears click into
gear.

———————————————

WHEN *I take my work one step at a time it is easy.*
Luckily, I can only do one step at a time anyway.

AWARENESS OF PROCESS/ COMMITMENT: STEP THREE

To believe in something not yet proved and to under-write it with our lives: it is the only way we can leave the future open.

—Lillian Smith

There once was a woman who said that she experienced the idea of Living in Process as akin to jumping off a cliff. Sometime after making that statement she related a dream in which she had come to the edge of a cliff and was aware of being very fearful of something coming up behind her. In the dream, she felt that she had only one positive choice—to jump off the cliff, which she did with great terror. Suddenly she was aware of a wonderful floating feeling. She opened her eyes and realized that her skirt had become a parachute: she was safe and floating comfortably.

"Leaving the future open" may be one of the most important commitments we make with our lives. Believing in something not yet proved may just be believing in ourselves.

WE NEVER KNOW *what will make good parachutes. When one is leaving the future open, it helps to know that there are parachutes not of our making in our lives.*

BECOMING/GETTING OLDER

We grow neither better or worse as we get old, but more like ourselves.

—Mary Lamberton Becker

I once met a woman in her sixties who shared what a marvelous revelation it was to her to become completely gray. "I can just put my ideas out the way I want to," she said, "and I don't get all of that strange sexual energy from men coming at me like I did when I was younger."

Another woman in her fifties confided that one of the best-kept secrets in this culture was what she called "post-menopausal zest." "I thought I was a whiz before menopause," she whispered conspiratorially, "and you should see me now."

These were obviously women who had chosen to let the process of aging facilitate their becoming more fully themselves.

——————————

AS THE DEMANDS *to falsify ourselves lessen, we can more easily concentrate on being the person we have always been.*

FEELING CRAZY

You were once wild here. Don't let them tame you!
— Isadora Duncan

We feel so overwhelmed by our feelings sometimes that we just feel like screaming. Women (and men!) do scream. We scream at our children, we scream at our spouses, we scream at our friends, and we scream at our employees. Often we and they attribute this behavior to the "time of the month" and write it off as crazy hormonal behavior. Down deep we feel ashamed, guilty, crazy, and unclean about this show of emotions.

Sometimes screaming is normal and necessary. We need to cry. We need to scream. It is part of our process and a normal response to living in a high-pressure, addictive society. However, we need *not* scream at others. We need to have our safe places where we can let our feelings out: have a good cry or have a good scream. This processing is normal for the human organism. We just believed that we were the only ones who needed it.

WHEN *I let my feelings out on others, I feel bad. When I just let my feelings out in a safe place, I feel good.*

FREEDOM

Sisterhood, like female friendship, has at its core the affirmation of freedom.

—Mary Daly

For women to be truly friends, we have to shed the suspicious competitiveness toward one another that we have been trained into. We have to move beyond seeing other women as competitors for the "goodies" (males and male validation and attention). We have to be open to the possibility that *because* we are women we have mutual concerns and experiences that we need to share. To do this, we have to be willing to move beyond our training and education for separateness, to leap the chasm and become free to be ourselves with one another.

Once we have made the leap, we find a richness and depth in our female friendships that simply is not possible with men. We find ourselves saying again and again, "I know," "I know." It is in "affirming our freedom" from old brainwashing that we move into friendship and sisterhood.

———————

THOUGH *I have been told otherwise, I need friends who are women.*

October 5

EMPTINESS

When one is a stranger to oneself, then one is estranged from others too.
—Anne Wilson Schaef

Whenever we stop long enough, we are aware of an inner feeling of emptiness. This feeling is so terrifying that we immediately get busy and try to block it out. We head for the refrigerator and attempt to bury it with food. We try to drown it with drink. We get very active with new projects or activities. We watch television.

If we just knew what we need to do to make this feeling go away, we would do it. We are competent women, and we can handle almost anything *when we know what it is*. All we really experience is the absence of something. We have a vague recollection that we once knew what it was, and we can't remember it now.

———————

MAYBE *what I'm missing is myself and my connection with my Higher Power.*

BEING OBSESSED

Why Women Who Do Too Much Housework Should Neglect It for Their Writing.
                                    —Brenda Ueland

This quotation is a chapter heading in Brenda Ueland's book *If You Want to Write*. It sums up the issue of being obsessed with our work. Yet she goes on to devote an entire chapter to it.

Why is it that the first things we give up and neglect are ourselves and the things that mean the most to us, like our creativity, our health, our children, and our loves? How sad it is that we often neglect our treasures for activities of far less value.

Well, that's what the insanity of addiction is about, isn't it? We cast our pearls into the pig pen, and we scrub the colors off the kitchen tiles.

———————

LET'S *get clear here about what needs to be neglected.*

BEING PRESENT TO THE MOMENT

Miracles are unexpected joys, surprising coincidences, unexplainable experiences, astonishing beauties . . . absolutely anything that happens in the course of my day, except that at this moment I'm able to recognize its special value.

—Judith M. Knowlton

Miracles are constantly occurring around us. Serendipities abound in daily life.

The issue is not that these miracles are absent. The issue is that often *we* are absent. We are standing on a hill of diamonds, and we are looking for the gold mine beyond the next ridge.

As we reclaim ourselves, we begin to notice the extraordinariness of the ordinary. We quit *thinking* about being present and we start doing it.

———————

THANK GOODNESS *I have walked in circles long enough to wear the soles of my shoes so thin that the diamonds on which I stand can now get my attention.*

Indispensable/Control

A few years ago, had someone called me an Indispensable Woman, I would have said, "Thank you." I would have considered it a compliment. Today, I know better.
—Ellen Sue Stern

As women who are caretakers and overworkers, we have often believed that we are indispensable. We have even made ourselves indispensable and then felt exhausted but secure. We believed that if the company, our children, our spouses, and our friends could not get along without us that there would always be a place for us in their lives. Our little hearts glowed when someone said, "What would I do without you?"

Thank goodness it *is* possible to teach an old dog new tricks! Many of us have seen that our indispensability not only was destructive to us, it was destroying all our relationships. We began to notice an undertone of resentment in those around us. People always resent those on whom they are dependent and those who try to control their lives.

I AM *so relieved that I discovered that being indispensable was killing me and my relationships. Now I have options!*

DESPAIR

A vacuum can only exist, I imagine, by the things that enclose it.

—Zelda Fitzgerald

A vacuum isn't just emptiness. It is the absence of something, and if it were not encased in its walls, a vacuum would not be possible.

We are familiar with the feeling of emptiness. There have been many times when we have felt that there just wasn't a drop of energy left in us. These periods are the "dark night of the soul." We will do anything to avoid feeling them; we even become addicted to whatever helps us not feel.

We have been trapped by the very lives we have designed. Our architectural wonders have become prefabricated horrors. Our enclosures are of our own making, and only we can dismantle them.

———————

JUST REMEMBER, *when a vacuum is opened up, many interesting possibilities rush in.*

CONFUSION

She's half-notes scattered without rhythm.
                                    —Ntozake Shange

We know that our lives have the potential of being a unique melody, and often they feel like "half-notes scattered without rhythm." When did the melody of our life go sour? Was it when we began to schedule more than we could handle? Was it when we began having difficulty relaxing? Was it when we began to feel resentful about the tasks we had agreed to do?

Sometime, probably gradually, our lives moved from concerto to crisis. The more we slip into this disease of doing too much, the more confused we become.

It is comforting to know that this confusion *is* part of the disease and recovery promises us the possibility of clarity.

———————

WHEN *I see my confusion as part of a progressive, fatal disease, I am not so hard on myself.*

MONOTONE MIND

I don't want to get to the end of my life and find that I just lived the length of it. I want to have lived the width of it as well.

—Diane Ackerman

When we become overly focused on our work, our children, our homes, or our relationships, we become one-dimensional women. Throughout history, and more recently with the women's movement, we have been painfully aware that women have often been limited to the more mindless tasks of the society.

Unfortunately, as more of us break in to the ranks of the privileged (as we have viewed them), we again find that we have the opportunity to become dull and narrow . . . just in a different way. The content has changed. The process remains the same.

In order to reclaim our souls, we need to recognize that width is as important as length in the living of our days.

WIDTH *adds a dimension to length. Depth adds a dimension to length and width. The world is at least three-dimensional.*

CONFUSED THINKING/ JUDGMENTALISM

I realize what a lot of negativity there is in the world and all around us, and how easy it is to become part of that negativity and to be sucked into it and become part of the chaos and confusion if one isn't very careful.
—Eileen Caddy

Negativity is one aspect of the typical confused thinking of the addict. The addictive disease feeds on these thinking processes. In our work lives, we are rewarded for analyzing, comparing, criticizing, and being negative. It is easy to see how we become sucked into negativity and the focus upon what's wrong. The key here is judgmentalism.

It's important to see what's wrong in any situation and what needs to be changed. When judgmentalism enters in, however, the observation takes on a tone of negativity, and that negativity is very seductive.

———————

LEARNING *to see clearly and not get sucked into confusion and negativity is one of the challenges of my recovery.*

CONTROL

When nothing is sure, everything is possible.
                                    —Margaret Drabble

These words strike terror in the heart of the woman who does too much. Even the prospect of admitting that nothing is sure stimulates our minds to get very busy listing the things in our lives that we are sure about. When we are honest, the list is very small: death is perhaps the only really *sure* thing. Everything else is merely possible.

One of the exciting wonders of recognizing our need for control and beginning to let it go is the weight-lessness of the anticipation that everything is possible. When we realize we don't know, we are open to what we don't know.

LIVING *by faith is flying by the seat of my pants. I'm really living that way anyway, but I have denied it as long as I could.*

FEELING OVERWHELMED

I feel like I'm fighting a battle when I didn't start a war.

—Dolly Parton

Sometimes we feel overwhelmed with forces outside ourselves. We find ourselves embroiled in family or organizational wars and infighting that we do not believe we started and that we certainly do not want to participate in. Yet once in them we feel as if we have to fight, or at least try to stop them.

Both behaviors feed such battles. The one thing we have the power to decide about is our participation. We have the power to decide *not* to participate. It is amazing how battles dissipate when no one participates. When we feel overwhelmed by the battle, we cannot see or we forgot that we have the power of nonparticipation.

————————

WARMONGERING *is common in an addictive workplace. I have a choice about my warmongering.*

BEAUTY

Because the best way to know the truth or beauty is to try to express it. And what is the purpose of existence here or yonder but to discover truth and beauty and express it, i.e., share it with others?
—Brenda Ueland

If the purpose of existence is to discover truth and beauty and share our discovery with others, some of us may have been on the wrong track.

In our need to achieve and move ahead, we have become stingy. As addicts, we believe that there is a limited amount of power and success and that if we give anything away, we will have less. So we develop the wonderful character defect of stinginess.

We have begun to think that if we share ideas or awareness, others will steal them. We censor, copyright, and choke our knowledge, and . . . we lose.

GREAT IDEAS *belong to everyone. It is only the small ones that have to be counted.*

BECOMING/CONTROL

*I also know that when I'm trusting and being myself
as fully as possible, everything in my life reflects this
by falling into place easily, often miraculously.*
—Shakti Gawain

We have been taught by the control system in which
we work and live that we have to fight, control, and
struggle to succeed. Consequently, we often end up
exhausted and bloody from our efforts.

We are convinced that just being ourselves cannot
possibly be enough. Yet as we get to know others who
are further along than we are in their recovery, we see
women who seem to do quite well by trusting and
being themselves. Their lives just seem to unfold.

THE UNFOLDING *of my life is not an issue of competence or control. It is an issue of faith.*

BEAUTY/ONENESS/AWE

Since you are like no other being ever created since the beginning of time, you are incomparable.
                                        —Brenda Ueland

When I read those words of Brenda Ueland, I take a deep breath and let it out very slowly. I am incomparable. Just letting myself truly know that elicits a feeling of awe and reverence . . . reverence for myself.

In Twelve-Step circles there is a concept of "terminal uniqueness." One is terminally unique when one believes that no one else has had it so bad and that we are the center of the universe. When we insist in defining the world from our own perspective, we are operating out of terminal uniqueness. Terminal uniqueness erodes the soul.

When we accept and celebrate our uniqueness, we take our place in the universe.

———————

THERE ARE *many things of beauty, and I am one of them!*

Awareness

There are no new truths, but only truths that have been recognized by those who have perceived them without noticing.

—Mary McCarthy

Our greatest learnings often come when we are unaware that we are learning something. We can study a technique or focus upon a project for days, and the truth or the essence of it just does not seem to click. Then something happens. The fog clears and we notice that we have moved to a new level of truth without ever knowing how we got there. It was not our straining or trying that brought us to this new level. It was our willingness to be aware of what had already taken place that opened new doors.

We do not control all the processes of our being. Sometimes we have but to notice. That is all.

———————

TODAY *has the potential of being a day in which I can recognize the truths working within me.*

JUSTIFICATION

*I use other addictions (eating, sex, drinking, spending)
to reward my workaholism.*

—Barb

"If I just get this project finished on time, I will take us
to that expensive new restaurant, and we will order
whatever we want on the whole menu."

"When I work so hard, I feel I deserve a drink or
two in the evening to relax me. After all, I have put in
a high-stress, productive day. I deserve to relax!"

"Sex is a good release. It gets too complicated if I
put extra baggage on it like love, communication, and
connectedness. Sometimes a woman just needs a release. This isn't using my partner. Partners have their
needs, too. Using each other for a release of tension
isn't *really* using each other."

I DO, *after all, have a right to my addictions. It's my
life, isn't it?*
Yes, it is!

October 20

AWARENESS OF PROCESS/CONTROL

Time is a dressmaker specializing in alterations.
                                            —Faith Baldwin

We often think that we are "just about to get it together" when life gives us another opportunity for
learning. Many of us have tried to treat our lives like
our houses. We have believed that we could get our
houses fixed up just the way we wanted them and then
they would stay that way forever. We have felt personally attacked when slip covers wear out, when a room
needs to be repainted, or when an appliance breaks
down. We have set up our lives based upon a static notion of the universe. We have believed that once fixed
things should stay fixed, whether they be our houses,
our jobs, or ourselves. In trying to make ourselves and
our universe static, we have set ourselves up for intense moments of frustration and failure. Our attempts to control the normal processes of life have
taken their toll on ourselves and those around us.

I AM *a process. Life is a process. Alterations are part of
the process.*

FEAR

While we wait in silence for that final luxury of fear-
lessness, the weight of that silence will choke us.
                                        —Audre Lorde

Our silence about the issues that matter most to us
thunders in our heads and bodies like a galloping herd
of buffalo. The canyons of our inner beings resound
with our unspoken ideas and perceptions.

Our fear confines our souls in the daily holocausts
of silent existence. Our fear is real. It is palpable. We
can feel it. We must learn to honor it and move
through it. We cannot deny it, and we cannot "wait for
that final luxury of fearlessness." To become fixated in
our fear is to creep in to that choking silence that devours our soul. No woman must speak when she is not
ready. We must respect one another in our silence.
When we face our fears, we may hear our voices.

MY FEAR *is real. I will honor it. And I do not need to*
be controlled by it.

October 22

AMENDS

I have refrained from speaking the truth and have just gone along with a lot of things.

—Marion Cohen

One of the most important steps in our recovery from our addiction to work, caretaking, rushing, and busyness is the amends process. First we need to make a list of those whom we have wronged. Then we need to make amends for our wrongs when it would not be harmful to do so.

It is important to remember that we make amends for ourselves. We do not make amends to get forgiveness. We do not make amends to make others like us. We do not make amends to control or manipulate.

We make amends because we need to do so in order to maintain our clarity and our sobriety. We make amends because it clears our soul to admit our wrongs, say we are sorry, and turn them over to a power greater than ourselves.

AMENDS-MAKING *is a way of vacuuming my soul. The result is, I feel clean.*

ACCEPTANCE/LIVING IN THE NOW

The opportunity of life is very precious and it moves very quickly.

—Ilyani Ywahoo

This is it! The life that is ours is the one we are living today. There is no other. The more we try to hold onto our illusions of what we *think* it is or what we think it *should* be, the less time and energy we have to live it.

How many times have we heard about people who worked hard and longed for the day when retirement would come, only to drop dead just before or just after they retired? How fast it all went!

Our lives are so precious. Each moment has the possibility of a new discovery. Yet when it passes, that moment never returns.

———————

ONLY AS I AM *aware of the present will I have the opportunity to be fully alive.*

PARENTING

If we try to control and hold onto our children, we lose them. When we let them go, they have the option of returning to us more fully.

——Anne Wilson Schaef

Few of us have a Ph.D. in parenting. If we did, we would probably be worse than we are now. How much energy we put into trying to mold and control our children, not for their sakes, but so they will reflect better on us.

We are unable to see them as separate and important beings who are here to share a time with us so that we can learn from each other. We think we *need* them to validate our lives and our choices in life. When we do that, we use them as objects, which is totally disrespectful of them and of ourselves.

———————————

TO LOVE *our children is to see them, respect them, share life with them . . . and always to let go.*

HOPES AND DREAMS

"Hope" is the thing with feathers
That perches in the soul . . .
And sings the tune without words
And never stops . . . at all
                                        —Emily Dickinson

It is nice to remember that we have a little feathered being deep in us that sings unceasingly.

So often, we believe that we have come to a place that is void of hope and void of possibilities, only to find that it is the very hopelessness that allows us to hit bottom, give up our illusion of control, turn it over, and ask for help. Out of the ashes of our hopelessness comes the fire of our hope.

To be without hopes and dreams is a place of loss . . . loss of our birthright as a human being. Hope does spring and sing eternal, even when we have wax in our ears.

———————————

BY RECOGNIZING *and affirming my feelings of hopelessness, I open the possibility of something else.*

October 26

IMPRESSION MANAGEMENT

*"The purpose of these workshops is to share . . . every-
thing we have learned from the dying patient who has
been our teacher . . . things that regrettably no one
helped them accomplish earlier so that they would
have been able to say, 'I have truly lived.'"*
—Elizabeth Kübler-Ross

From many years of helping the terminally ill to re-
solve their unfinished business in this life, Dr. Kübler-
Ross knows better than most how many things get in
the way of our experiencing fully what it means to
live. One major block we often use is impression management.

Trying to be what others want us to be is a form of
slow torture and certain spiritual death. It is not possible to get all our definitions from outside and maintain our spiritual integrity. We cannot look to others
to tell us who we are, give us our validity, give us our
meaning, and still have any idea of who we are. When
we look to others for our identity, we spend most of
our time and energy trying to be who they want us to
be. And we are so fearful of being found out. We truly
believe that it is possible to make others see what we
want them to see, and we exhaust ourselves in the
process.

IMPRESSION MANAGEMENT *is a form of the illusion of control and I know that my illusion of control
will kill me.*

CREATIVITY

It is the creative potential itself in human beings that is the image of God.

—Mary Daly

What a beautiful way to think of our creativity! If we do not express our creativity, we are blocking the potential of the flowing energy of the image of God.

For most women who do too much, creativity has a very low place in our list of priorities. We don't have time to be creative. We will be creative later (and later . . . and later). We don't really believe in *our* creativity. Only special women have real creativity, and we are so terrified that we may not be one of these women that we won't even try to see what *our* creativity is. After all, "If you can't do something outstanding, it's better not to do anything at all."

WHEN I THINK *of my creative potential as the "image of God" within me, I feel awe.*

COMMUNICATION

The only listening that counts is that of the talker
who alternately absorbs and expresses ideas.
—Agnes Repplier

Women have historically been good listeners. We have been trained to listen carefully and even to "listen with the third ear." Caretakers need to listen, often not saying what they think they need to say.

As we have become women who do too much, we find our listening skills on the wane. We cut people off in the middle of sentences. We assume we know what an employee is going to say, and we act on that assumption. We even become enamored with the sound of our own voice.

We must remember that communication is more than a monologue. Good communication is a balance of speaking and sharing, listening carefully, and absorbing before we speak again.

We as women often limit ourselves to listening or talking. Thus we miss the meaning of communication.

––––––––––––––

TODAY *I have the opportunity to observe if I practice all three aspects of communication.*

ONENESS

> *To the Indian mind, the life of the universe has not been analyzed, classified, and a great synthesis formed of the parts. To him [sic] the varied forms are equally important and varied.*
>
> —Alice C. Fletcher

Recently, I heard a woman discussing why she enjoyed spending part of her time with an elderly woman friend in a household of women. "Everything gets done so easily," she said. "All the jobs have equal status. Washing the clothes or cooking a meal has just as much status as the work we do in our offices as physicians. It all just flows."

I was reminded of how much we analyze our universe, assign random values, and chop up our lives. That process not only makes our lives more difficult, it alienates us from the experience of oneness with all things, and without that experience, we don't know that we belong.

———

WHEN *I diminish other's belongingness in the universe,* my *belongingness becomes uncertain.*

BEING OBSESSED/NEEDING OTHERS

She who rides a tiger is afraid to dismount.
—Proverb

Being obsessed with our work is often thought to be a requirement for success. Yet, when was it that the tail started wagging the dog? Where was the point at which we stopped doing our work, and it began doing us?

It is a lot harder to get off the roller coaster in the middle than it was to get on it. This is why we need the companionship of others who are struggling with the same issues: they support our process of getting unhooked from our obsessive doing.

It is only with the support of others and the renewed connection with a power greater than ourselves that we can hope to recover and become whole.

I SUPPOSE *I can dismount if I have a few people holding the tiger.*

October 31

BEING PROJECTLESS

How beautiful it is to do nothing, and then rest afterward.

—Spanish proverb

For many of us the thought of doing nothing is terrifying. We cannot imagine what life would be like if we were not slaving away at our projects. Not to have our projects waiting for us is like trying to live with parts missing. We have become so dependent upon the security of the next project that they are no longer *our* projects. We are owned by them.

Workaholics often experience some depression when they complete a task. Instead of dealing with the natural feeling of letdown, we overlap completion with a new beginning. Hence, like the relationship addict, we never have to deal with separation or beginnings and endings. In fact, we never have to deal with anything.

PERHAPS TODAY *I could experiment with doing nothing, and resting afterward.*

WORK/CAUSES

Beware of people carrying ideas. Beware of ideas carrying people.
— Barbara Grizzuti Harrison

Ideas can be so seductive, and we are so easily seduced. We forget that ideas are just that, abstractions that have been thought up.

We often lose ourselves in ideas and become so caught up in them that we cannot distinguish between ourselves and the idea. When we reach this level of enmeshment with our ideas, we experience any attack on our ideas as an attack on our being.

Being so attached to our ideas often results in a widening gap between what we are espousing and what we actually do. How often we kill in the name of love. We talk about cooperation and we try to force it on others. We get an idea for high productivity and we interfere with productivity by demanding an adherence to our idea. We start out carrying an idea and soon it is carrying us.

———————

I WILL NOT *let what I think destroy what I believe.*

GUILT

*Who I am is what I have to give. Quite simply, I must
remember that's enough.*
—Anne Wilson Schaef

Often, when we look in our inner recesses, we feel
that we are lacking. We have been a disappointment
to others. We couldn't "be there" when we should
have been, and we didn't have all the information we
should have had. Somehow, though it may be just a
vague feeling, we have failed.

It appears that feeling guilty is a sex-linked gene.
There seems to be an infinitely close connection between feeling guilty and being female.

When we feel guilty, we try to make up for what
we have or have not done. We feel we need to "make
something special," to make things all right. We need
to make up for a "transgression" even if we don't
know what it was. Unfortunately, our technique for
making up is usually addictive and not good for us or
the person to whom we give it.

———————————

I CANNOT *make up for something I think I haven't
done or have done wrong by trying to make others or
myself feel guilty.*

November 3

CRISIS ORIENTATION

> *The Physician says I have "Nervous*
> *prostration."*
> *Possibly I have—I do not know the names of*
> *sickness. The crisis*
> *of the sorrow of so many years is all that*
> *tires me.*
>
> *—Emily Dickinson*

Physicians have invented many erudite and confounding names for women who work themselves to a complete frazzle. We spend our lives moving from one crisis to another. As a matter of fact, we have become so competent at handling crisis that we feel most at home in the middle of one. If the truth were known, we women who do too much often create a crisis when things are going smoothly. When things are quiet, we keep waiting for the other shoe to fall and we feel relieved when we have a crisis to be managed. We know how to do that.

———————————

SERIAL CRISES *are exciting,* and *they are exhausting. I don't want crises to be the origin of yet another medical label. Recovery offers another option.*

November 4

CONTROL/RECOVERY

You know you're recovering when you can go to a family reunion and you don't have to teach, preach, or leave literature.

—Karen

A big part of our disease is believing that we not only have the right answers for ourselves but for other people as well. Our investment in this belief is such that we truly believe that we can make other people think and behave as we want. And we actually believe that it is right to do so, since we know best.

How arrogant we have become in our illusion of control! How disrespectful of others to try to control their lives and convince them of what is best for them! How much easier it is to work *with* people instead of trying to overpower them with the righteousness of our rightness. Control is deadly for everyone.

I WILL REMEMBER *that my illusion of control is just that . . . an illusion.*

FINANCIAL SECURITY

*It seems that the rewards of an affluent society turn
bitter as gall in the mouth.*
                                    ——Natalie Shaeness

An affluent society often functions as a giant tranquil-
izer. In the pursuit of the rewards of affluence, we
have to tune out our awareness so completely that we
become destructive to our bodies and our psyches.
We have to develop our addictions to shut off our
awareness of what is *really* important to us. We operate out of denial and are threatened by anyone wanting to challenge our denial.

When we see the sole purpose of our work as the
pursuit of affluence, we have lost track of ourselves
and what is meaningful work for us. Our spiritual
selves have become an abstraction, if they exist at all.

GALL *is useful for digesting fats and reducing the risk
of heart attack. It is useless in the mouth.*

Deadlines/Procrastination

The shortest answer is doing.
                                    —English proverb

Although we women who do too much do overwork and overextend ourselves, we also struggle with procrastination. Just let a deadline approach, and we slip in to the sloughs of lethargy. We just can't get ourselves going. Working at a steady pace is not our style. We work in spurts: intense crisis-mode operating and then nothing. Just thinking about deadlines exhausts us. Meeting them wipes us out.

Deadlines are a threat to the sobriety of the recovering workaholic. They offer us an opportunity to slip back into our old patterns. Remember, relapse is just as dangerous for a workaholic as it is for an alcoholic. We both have a progressive, fatal disease.

Deadlines offer us the opportunity to reach out and ask for support. Talking with our sponsor is a necessary facet of our recovery.

THIS DEADLINE *is a gift to help me see how much progress I have made and how I can function differently.*

November 7

COURAGE

What I am actually saying is that we each need to let our intuition guide us, and then be willing to follow that guidance directly and fearlessly.
— Shakti Gawain

One of the most frightening things in the world is to trust our intuition and follow that trusting. It is hard for us to believe that what the Quakers call our "inner light" is really the way our power greater than ourselves speaks most clearly to us.

When we are one with ourselves and our process, we are truly one with the process of the universe. When we are one with ourselves, our lives seem to fall into place effortlessly. All of us know the feeling of moments of effortless living. When we have the courage to trust our intuition, life begins to live itself.

MY INTUITION *connects me with the voice I need to hear.*

November 8

ACTION

There is really nothing more to say—except why. But since why is difficult to handle, one must take refuge in how.

—Toni Morrison

There are often events in our lives that just do not make sense. In spite of our best efforts, projects fail. It is important to take stock of the situation and accept our part in the failure and then move on.

When we get stuck on the why, we can stay stuck for a long time. We so want to understand, and it is so difficult to admit that some things just make no sense. In Twelve-Step circles, people say, "Whying is dying."

Faith in living does not ask why. Faith in living asks how and does it.

THE EVENT *may not be the problem. Our need to understand it may be the problem.*

November 9

HANGING IN/STUBBORNNESS

*It is not true that life is one damn thing after another
. . . it's the same damn thing over and over again.*
                    —Edna St. Vincent Millay

Our inner process gives us every opportunity to learn
what we need to learn. Our inner being is very conservation minded—it continues to recycle our shit,
and recycles our shit, and recycles our shit. If we don't
get the lesson the first time around, we get another
chance . . . and another . . . and another. Life gives us
every opportunity to work through whatever we need
to work through.

Unfortunately, every time an opportunity for learning recycles, it comes with a greater and greater force.
The intensity of the force with which we have to be hit
is directly related to our denial, stubbornness, and illusion of control. Life will cycle the same damn thing
over and over again, until we get it.

———————————

I'M GLAD *my inner process hangs in with me. Sometimes I'm a slow learner.*

LETTING GO/CONTROL

> *The true secret of giving advice is, after you have hon-*
> *estly given it, to be perfectly indifferent whether it is*
> *taken or not and never persist in trying to set people*
> *right.*
>
> —Hannah Whitall Smith

Actually, we probably should never give advice, even when someone asks for it. However, it is often helpful to give information and then *let it go*. Too often we get invested in our information and are so sure of our rightness that we have to make certain the other person *accepts* it. Somehow, deep inside of us their acceptance of our information is directly tied to our self-worth. If they don't accept our advice and act on it, we are somehow not liked, respected, valued, and a whole string of other adjectives.

As we get healthier and begin to give up some of our addictive behaviors, we find that our need to control others is lessening. We are learning to give and let go.

I HAVE *good information to share. It is more likely to be heard when I give it and let it go.*

BUSYNESS/CAUSES/AWARENESS

Why is it that when people have no capacity for private usefulness they should be so anxious to serve the public?

— Sara Jeanette Duncan

How many of us use our causes and our projects as a front for our addiction to our busyness? Do we impose ourselves and our views on others as a way of not having to look inside?

Causes look so noble, and serving the public seems so pure. Are nobility and purity really what we are about? Is our need for power and recognition related to our feelings of unworthiness? I wonder how honest we are with ourselves about the real motivation behind our causes and our service. We may only be developing subtle, more socially acceptable ways of practicing our disease. We do have options, however.

AWARENESS *is the key. When I know what I am doing, I have the option to change.*

CREATIVITY

As soon as I began painting what was in my head the people around me were shocked.

—Leonor Fini

Our creativity, once unleashed, knows no time or space. It is like a passionate lover that demands to be heard. No wonder we are so afraid of it. It can turn our world topsy-turvy. And maybe our worlds *need* to be turned topsy-turvy.

When our creativity shows itself, it is now. The ideas we are having now are a result of who we are now, our life situations now, and what is going on inside us now. We will not be the same women fifteen years from now.

Expressing our creativity now in whatever form it takes is a way of enriching our lives, making us more interesting women, and releasing the tension of not creating.

I OWE IT *to myself to find time for my creative self.*

November 13

DEMANDING TOO MUCH

If you knew how often I say to myself: to hell with every-thing, to hell with everybody, I've done my share, let the others do theirs now, enough, enough, enough.
　　　　　　　　　　　　　　—Golda Meir

Before we began to get healthier, we always were the first to go the extra mile. We were sure we were in-dispensable and if we didn't handle each situation, no one would.

Now we have a different perspective. When we get to a point where we feel like saying "to hell with everything," we know that the issue is not "out there," it is "in here" and that we have not been taking care of ourselves. When we take care of ourselves, we quit before we are forced to our knees. Working our re-covery program has taught us to be alert to the signs of self-neglect.

_____

I'M NOT *there yet. As I pay attention to the signals I give myself, I'm getting better and better.*

CONTROL

I was torn by two different time concepts. I knew which one made sense, but the other one was fighting hard for survival. [Structure, regimentation, orderedness. Which had absolutely nothing to do with anything.]
—Robyn Davidson

One of the ways we practice our illusion of control and protect our disease is to surround ourselves with people like ourselves who do the same things we do. When we are surrounded by women who also rush around, are always busy, work too much, and take care of everyone, we seem normal. Our addictions seem normal. We avoid putting ourselves in situations where our control skills are not shared and valued, because then in that situation we might notice that we do not like controlling at all. Structure, regimentation, and orderedness are the way things have to be, or so we believe. That is why when we do allow ourselves to travel, we stay in American hotels with well-known names, if possible.

———————

OUR ILLUSION *of control is more cunning than a cat, and it has more than nine lives.*

November 15

ACCEPTANCE/CONTROL/
SERENITY PRAYER

*Now I think my point is that I have learned to live
with it all . . . with being old . . . whatever happens
. . . all of it.*

—Edelgard

How wonderful that we not only have the opportunity to live our lives, we have the opportunity to *accept* them! We have spent so much time and energy foolishly fighting things that we cannot change and butting our heads up against steel-reinforced brick walls that we have not stopped to ask ourselves if this is the hill we want to die on.

Part of learning to live our lives is developing the ability to accept what cannot be changed and learn to live creatively with those situations. Also, we need to discover what can be challenged and to move forward with courage when necessary. Acceptance is not resignation. Acceptance is serenity embracing life.

———————

TODAY *my life is enough just the way it is,* and *it is mine.*

FEELING CRAZY

STEPS ONE, TWO, AND THREE

Crazy and coping are interactive. They go together and are mutually supportive. When I'm crazy, I believe I have to cope and when I am trying to cope, I get crazy.
— Karen M.

The crazier we feel, the more we feel we should be able to cope. That's part of the progression of this disease: we lose our ability to make clear and sane judgments about ourselves and the situations in which we find ourselves. We find ourselves trying to accomplish feats that no sane person would even attempt and fully expecting that we should be able to accomplish them with great ease. In fact, our progressively taking on more and more is directly related to our creeping closer to the brink. It is difficult to tell which is the chicken and which is the egg—probably neither. They are interactive. Our taking on more and more drives us closer and closer to the brink and getting closer and closer to the brink results in our taking on more and more.

———————

INERTIA *is the force that keeps an object at rest when at rest or in motion when in motion, unless acted upon by an external force.*

We have an inertia problem. We need an outside force. We can't do this by ourselves.

SELF-AWARENESS

There's a period of life when we swallow a knowledge
of ourselves and it becomes either good or sour inside.
—Pearl Bailey

Self-knowledge is always a good thing. No one else possesses the capacity to know us as well as we can know ourselves.

It is in the awareness of ourselves that our strength lies. And awareness of every aspect of ourselves allows us to become who we are.

Often our rejection of various aspects of ourselves keeps us stuck. Some of us quite readily see those aspects of our personalities that we perceive as negative and just as readily beat ourselves up for those characteristics. Others go to the other extreme and sugar-coat our self-perceptions, putting all blame and responsibility for who we have become on anyone and anything outside of ourselves. Neither approach is helpful or growth-producing.

———————————

OWNING *ourselves is probably the richest gold mine*
any of us will ever possess.

ACCEPTANCE/AMBITION

> *I long to accomplish a great and noble task, but it is
> my chief duty to accomplish small tasks as if they were
> great and noble.*
>
> —Helen Keller

Such amazing words from a person whose life in itself
was such "a great and noble task"! In Helen Keller's
words we sense such deep acceptance of her life. We
have a glimmer of insight into the paradox that if we
just take one step at a time and do each task as it presents itself, we may discover we have done great and
noble things. If we are *trying* to do great and noble
tasks, we may well find that we have missed those
magic opportunities just to do what we need to do.

As the author Brenda Ueland says, "Try to discover
your true, honest, untheoretical self." Our theoretical
self often interferes with our real self.

MY ILLUSION *of myself may not be who I am. My
illusion of my work may not be what it is.*

November 19

TIME MANAGEMENT

I'm working so hard on my time management that I don't get anything done.

—Anonymous

We can get so involved in a new technique that the technique itself becomes another monster in our lives, and we become slaves to it.

Time management can be a good thing. It can help us look at how we spend our time. It can help us become more efficient in getting a job done and can help us learn new ways of doing old things. None of us is as efficient as we could be, and efficiency is useful.

However, when we use any technique to support our disease of workaholism, that technique becomes part of the problem. Unfortunately, addicts are good at using anything to support the disease.

When we are recovering, we have a better perspective for evaluating our use of such tools to make our lives more serene and healthy.

I WILL BE OPEN *to tools for recovery, recognizing that the Twelve Steps of Workaholics Anonymous are some of the best tools available.*

APPRECIATION

You must not think that I feel, in spite of it having ended in such defeat, that my "life has been wasted" here, or that I would exchange it with that of anyone I know.

—Isak Dinesen

One of the most important aspects of our lives is that they are *our* lives. No one else could live them exactly the way we are living them. Everything that happens in our lives is an opportunity for learning. Those moments of frustration often turn into moments of joy and creativity.

What an extraordinary experience it is to look back and truly feel that we can celebrate our lives—all of them.

Being in recovery and returning to our spiritual selves provides a path to appreciation.

———————————

I HAVE *the opportunity to walk the path of appreciation today.*

ALONE TIME

Women's normal occupations in general run counter to creative life or contemplative life or saintly life.
—Anne Morrow Lindbergh

There is not much in our lives that supports our creativity. Work in the home and work outside the home are generally not conducive to the kind of nurturing that every human being needs. As we buy into the workaholism, competitiveness, and stress of the dominant society, we find ourselves changing and losing many of the qualities that were most precious to us.

We have rebelled against women's work, and we have raced headlong into men's work. Now we not only get to do women's work, we get to do both and work twice as hard.

We find our moments of creative time or contemplative time, or even saintly time, are few and far between. Yet, we need these times and we deserve these times for ourselves.

———————

I WILL TRY *to remember that when I take time for myself, I have much more to offer to myself, my work, and those around me.*

November 22

WHOLENESS

Women's work is always toward wholeness.
—May Sarton

When we women do *our* work, we move toward wholeness. The world is in need of wholeness. The world is in need of women's way of working.

Too long we have doubted ourselves and tried to fit comfortably into a male modality. To have wholeness, we need to make our contribution too. To have wholeness, we need to know our values and value our knowing.

We have reneged on our responsibility to this society and this planet. It is time that we courageously put our thoughts, ideas, and values out there and let them stand for themselves.

———————————

WHEN I DO *my work, my work is wholeness.*

TURNING IT OVER

I need to take an emotional breath, step back, and re-
mind myself who's actually in charge of my life.
                                        —Judith M. Knowlton

How often we want to stop, turn around angrily, and
shout, *"who's in charge here?"* We have tried to be in
charge of our lives and have learned again and again
that our being in charge has not quite worked. Sooooo
. . . if we aren't, who is?

It seems too nebulous for a practical, professional
woman just to step back and turn her life over to
some vague power that may exist out there. Isn't reli-
gion for weaklings? Aren't those who want to depend
upon a power greater than themselves just being dependent and not taking responsibility for themselves?
Perhaps. Yet, when we think dualistically like that,
when we grab the power or we give it up, we miss the
point.

Life is a process of cooperating with the forces in
our lives and living out that partnership.

WE ARE *in charge together. Not as controllers . . . as*
a living process.

November 24

SOLITUDE

Like water which can clearly mirror the sky and the trees only so long as its surface is undisturbed, the mind can only reflect the true image of the Self when it is tranquil and wholly relaxed.

—Indra Devi

How often are our minds "tranquil and wholly relaxed"? Do we recognize that time for solitude is just as important to our work as keeping informed, preparing reports, or planning? As author Brenda Ueland says, "Presently your soul gets frightfully sterile and dry because you are so quick, snappy and efficient about doing one thing after another that you have no time for your own ideas to come in and develop and gently shine."

We have to give ourselves time. We have to give our ideas time. If we don't neither we nor they can gently shine, and we cannot hear the voice of our inner process speaking to us.

SOLITUDE *is not a luxury. It is a right and a necessity.*

November 25

PERFECTIONISM

Don't try to be such a perfect girl, darling. Do the best you can without too much anxiety or strain.
— Jesse Barnard

How many of us have longed for words from our mothers like the ones Jesse Barnard wrote to her daughter. Perhaps, if our parents hadn't needed us to be perfect, *we* wouldn't need to be perfect. Unfortunately, even when others do not demand perfection of us, we who do too much demand it of ourselves.

We forget that when push comes to shove the only standard of perfection we have to meet is to be perfectly ourselves. Whenever we set up abstract, external standards and try to force ourselves to meet them, we destroy ourselves.

DOING THE BEST *I can without too much anxiety or strain sounds like a relaxing way to live.*

REACHING OUT: STEP TWELVE

May our Mayness become All-embracing. May we see in one another the All that was once All-one rebecome One.

—Laura Riding

Part of the beauty of recovering from doing too much is realizing that our lives are changing and that we seem to be taking on a more spiritual quality despite ourselves.

Also, as we stop working ourselves to death, we find that we have more time to reach out to others and that the very act of reaching out seems to be good for us and, surprisingly, seems to facilitate our growth and recovery.

We grow beyond wanting to fix others. We realize that sharing our journey toward recovery with others is one of the ways we remember our stories, remember where we have been, remember who we are, and progress in our recovery.

———————

WHEN WE REACH OUT *to another, we have the possibility of remembering that we are one, we are the same.*

November 27

HAPPINESS

If you haven't been happy very young, you still can be happy later on, but it's much harder, you need more luck.

—Simone de Beauvoir

We all carry influences and experiences from our childhood into our adult lives. Dysfunctional families are the norm for this society and probably the question is not, Do we have something that needs to be worked out from our childhood? The appropriate question probably is, What do we have to work on from the experiences of our childhood?

The amazing thing about the human adventure is that no matter how horrendously awful our childhood was, as we work through it, we always find some memories of moments of happiness that had long since been forgotten. And no matter how perfect our family seemed on the surface, we always have some painful experiences to work through.

TRUE HAPPINESS *does not come from a perfect childhood. Happiness comes from claiming our unique childhood and working through the lessons it holds for us.*

IN TOUCH WITH A POWER GREATER THAN OURSELVES

It is not primarily abstract ideas which affect our spirituality, that is, our experience of and with God.
—Sandra M. Schneiders

We cannot approach God or the process of the universe through ideas. Theology is trying to think out God and often asking us to deny our *experience* of a power greater than ourselves.

When we learn to trust our own perceptions and experience, we discover that we begin to have a relationship with the process of the universe. In fact, as we do our recovery work, we discover that when we are living out of our own process, we are one with the universe. We are the holomovement.

This living process that is us is, at the same time, greater than ourselves. When we are truly ourselves, we are more than ourselves. We do not have to look for spirituality. We *are* spirituality.

————————

MY EXPERIENCE *of the infinite cannot begin with my head.*

November 29

LAUGHTER

One loses many laughs by not laughing at oneself.
—Sara Jeannette Duncan

Well said! Part of the recovery process is to be able to see how really funny we are in our disease. We take ourselves so seriously.

One of my better moments was when I was invited to be the guest speaker at an important luncheon for one of the Fortune Five Hundred corporations. I had been out camping just prior to this speaking engagement, so I felt a little seedy. In order to make the right impression, I had brought a conservative business suit, silk blouse, high heeled boots, and panty hose. After being in the wilderness for some time, I wasn't even sure I knew how to get into this garb. Just before it was time to speak, I went to the bathroom to "pee my anxieties down the toilet" as we say in clinical circles. I came out of the bathroom feeling a little cocky and ready to go. Just as I reached the door to the auditorium, I was aware of a breeze and realized that my skirt was caught up in my panty hose and my rear was "exposed to the rockies." I had an instant opportunity for humility. Of course it made a great opener for my speech.

WHEN WE SEE *how funny we are, we see how dear we are.*

GUILT

Women keep a special corner of their hearts for sins they have never committed.

—Cornelia Otis Skinner

We are so ready to take responsibility for everything that we are constantly feeling guilty.

If our spouse is feeling down or depressed it must be something we have done. If our children aren't doing well, it must be our fault. If the deadline isn't met, we should have put in more time. Women are so ready to take on the guilt of the world. It makes no difference whether we have committed these transgressions. If they exist, we must be responsible. Unfortunately, there are plenty of people around us who are happy to support us in these illusions of guilt.

We have never really stopped to see how self-centered it is to take on the responsibility for everything that happens, whether we are involved or not. When we take on the guilt for everything that happens around us, we make ourselves the center of everything.

———————————

THERE MUST *be an easier way to be included.*

FINANCIAL SECURITY

Actually we are slaves to the cost of living.
                              —Carolina Marin deJesus

All of us have to cope with the cost of living. Existing gets more and more expensive, and living seems sometimes as if it is only for the wealthy.

We have lost track of the difference between what we want and what we need. Everything has become a need. If we don't have what we think we need, it lowers our self-esteem and our feelings of worth. We can hardly remember what is important anymore.

We are important. Our children are important. Our relationships are important. The planet is important. Our lives are important.

———————————

LEST WE FORGET *what we are all about, let's stop today and remember.*

INTERESTS/OVEREXTENDED

I am involved in so many things—both purely practical and also where my feelings, my life itself are concerned—possibly by my own fault or perhaps quite by chance, that it is going to take all my strength if I am going to get through them or over them.

—Isak Dinesen

Sometimes women who do too much get confused between healthy excitement about our work, a passion for our work, and workaholism. Passion moves to workaholism when it becomes destructive to the self and others. Workaholism isn't pursuing our interests. Workaholism doesn't give us time for our interests.

We often may overextend ourselves in the pursuit of our interests and the workaholic doesn't know when to stop. She just piles on more and more. The woman who has a healthy relationship with her interests is able to give her interests the time they deserve and savor them.

———————

MY INTERESTS *add richness to my life, but not when I go after them compulsively.*

December 3

FREEDOM

We must get in touch with our own liberating ludi-crousness and practice being harmlessly deviant.
                                    —Sarah J. McCarthy

Freedom for me means being who I am. Professional women are supposed to have short, neat hair. I have long hair which has a mind of its own. It's harmless . . . and it's me. It is, indeed, liberating to be "ludi-crous" and harmlessly deviant.

I once was a speaker at a university and while on campus was invited to attend a luncheon for the women faculty and staff on campus. During my lun-cheon speech, I asked if there was a dress code. I was quickly assured that the students could wear whatever they wanted. I told them I was asking about the women who worked on campus. They were all dressed exactly alike—suits, shirts, and some form of little tie. The only deviant was one woman who had a ruffle on her shirt!

———————————

FREEDOM *is choosing the clothing that fits our per-sonalities and feels good on us. This is one way we ex-press who we are.*

GIFTS

"We cannot find peace if we are afraid of the wind-storms of life."
                                                        —Elizabeth Kübler-Ross

Our lives don't always go smoothly. In fact, many of us have had many traumas and struggles. When we are in the midst of a difficult time, it is hard to see it as a gift. Nevertheless, at some mega level, every experience is an opportunity for learning.

When we spend our energy blaming and complaining, we are handing over our power to those whom we blame. Our time and energy is well spent when we stop and say, "What is my part in this situation, and what do I have to learn from it?" In doing this, we are not blaming ourselves. We are not blaming at all. We are opening ourselves to glean whatever learnings are there for us. It is in this process that we become whole.

I MAY NOT *always like the gift wrapping, and it's the gift that is important.*

BEING IN CHARGE

*Our strength is often composed of the weakness we're
damned if we're going to show.*
—Mignon McLaughlin

How in the world did I get to be in charge? There
must be some mistake. I don't know what to do with
this contract. I don't know how to raise these kids. I
must have misrepresented myself for "them" to believe that I knew what I was doing. I am secretly at my
best when someone else has the ultimate responsibility. Who has made this terrible mistake?

Often we truly believe that there must be someone
who really has it all together and knows just what to
do in every situation. Where is that person anyway?
Maybe we can ask the right questions and get the right
information, and then no one will suspect our cha-
rade.

———————————

YOU'RE IT, HONEY. *Go for it.*

December 6

COURAGE/OPENNESS/FEAR

To appreciate openness, *we must have experienced encouragement to try the new, to seek alternatives, to view fresh possibilities.*

—Sister Mary Luke Tobin

Courage and openness go hand in hand. Our courage helps us to take the risk to "try the new." When we are fearful, we only see one way, our way. Courage opens the way for new possibilities.

As we face our fears, we find that we are endowed with a level of courage that we never knew existed. Fortunately, we do not have to be a hero to demonstrate courage. We have many possibilities every day to act courageously. It takes courage to germinate and put forth new ideas. It takes courage to stand up for what we know in our hearts is right. Sometimes it even takes courage to take a nap.

———————

EVERYDAY COURAGE *is all I ask.*

CLIMBING THE LADDER

The best careers advice to give the young is, find out what you like doing best and get someone to pay you for doing it.

—Katherine Whilehaen

What we love doing often has no connection with our career choice. We live in a culture that teaches us to orient ourselves to what will sell. We have learned to ignore what we love and turn ourselves into a commodity. Commodities can be bought and sold, and we fear that we can be bought and sold. We don't feel that we have the luxury to see what it is we really want to be doing.

We forget one very central and essential factor: if we are doing what we love, we will probably do it exceedingly well.

———————————

IF WE FOCUS *on success, we will probably forget about living. If we focus on living and doing what we love, we have a good chance of being successful.*

December 8

SHARING
STEP TWELVE

When one's own problems are unsolvable and all best efforts are frustrated, it is lifesaving to listen to other people's problems.

—Suzanne Massie

Sometimes we just reach an impasse in our lives. In spite of our intelligence, competence, and tenacity, we just do not seem to be able to pull our lives together. Often times, this is where the wisdom of the Twelfth Step in the Twelve-Step program of Alcoholics Anonymous comes into play in our lives.

Because we have begun to be in touch with our spirituality and because we have begun to experience the healing of the Twelve-Step program, we are ready to share our strength and hope with others. Yet, when we do this, we are not reaching out in a self-centered way and we must simultaneously realize that when we reach out we often receive great benefit.

WHEN I AM *at an impasse in my life, I do not feel very strong. That may be just the time when reaching out to another is just what I need.*

December 9

CONFUSION/BUSYNESS

As a workaholic, I have learned that I have even worked the Twelve Steps of Alcoholics Anonymous workaholically: Yeah!! Yeah!! Fix those addictions!! Work those steps!! Rah! Rah!

—Michelle

Part of the subtlety of this disease is taking something that is good for us and doing it in such a way that it is destructive and perpetuates the problem.

Work is good. But if we do it compulsively and batter ourselves and those we love with it, it becomes destructive. Exercise is good. But if we use it to destroy our bodies, avoid intimacy, and keep out of touch with ourselves, it can have the same effect as heavy drinking.

At some deeper level in our lives, *how* we do things is just as important as *what* we do.

———————

WHEN *I destroy or punish myself with good things, I am still destroying or punishing myself.*

FEELING TRAPPED

> *Women are the slave class that maintains the species in order to free the other half for the business of the world.*
>
> —Shulamith Firestone

We wanted to become professional women partly because we wanted to remove ourselves from being the "slave class that maintains the species." Yet, it is difficult fully to escape that trap. We find that any job can become a trap, whether we are full-time homemakers, volunteers, support personnel, or executive-level managers. Our society is set up in such a way that it takes a great many to support the work of a few. And even if we are part of the few, we are not always free.

We need to recognize that all of us, regardless of what we do, are part of the "business of the world," and the world needs all of us.

————————————————

ACCEPTING *who I am and what I have to offer is empowering to me and the society.*

EXPECTATIONS

Know that if you have a kind of cultured know-it-all in yourself who takes pleasure in pointing out what is not good, in discriminating, reasoning, and comparing, you are bound under a knave. I wish you could be delivered.

—Brenda Ueland

We don't need anyone else to criticize us. We have so many superhuman expectations of ourselves that the expectations of others pale into insignificance. We really believe that we should be able to handle everything. We really believe we should know everything. We really believe that we should be on top of everything. When we are caught unprepared, instead of just admitting it, we either get defensive or feel guilty (or both). It rarely occurs to us just to admit we are unprepared. We feel we should always be prepared for anything. (No control issues here!)

OUR EXPECTATIONS *keep us from crying "uncle" (or for any other relative help, for that matter).*

RESPONSIBILITY

Take your life in your own hands, and what happens?
A terrible thing: no one to blame.

—Erica Jong

Women have been reluctant to take responsibility for our lives because we have been taught that responsibility means to be held accountable for what has happened to us and therefore to be blamed. Unfortunately, in reacting against this idea of responsibility we have missed the opportunity to own and claim our lives and thus have left ourselves without roots, ties, and understanding. We need to own our lives. We need to claim our experiences, all of them, and integrate them into our existence and decisions. We need to claim who we are and be who we are. That does not mean that we are to blame for our experiences. It means that we have before us the option of living our lives and not leaving that pleasure up to someone else.

———————————

WHEN *I take responsibility for my life, I have the ability to respond to all of it.*

BECOMING

One is not born a woman, one becomes one.
                                    —Simone de Beauvoir

We live in a society that puts so much emphasis upon youth, looks, and attractiveness that we have very few models for womanliness.

Without knowing how to get there, we are suddenly expected to be women and to have the wisdom and stature of a woman.

In a society that knows little about process, there is an assumption that one is a little girl and then suddenly one is a woman. In our sexualized culture, becoming a woman almost always is linked to our sexuality. Womanhood is much more than being sexual and producing babies. Womanhood is the progressive process of bringing all we have to offer as persons to ourselves and those around us.

———————

I AM *being a woman. That is a process, not a state.*

STRENGTH

From a timid, shy girl I had become a woman of resolute character, who could no longer be frightened by the struggle with troubles.

—Anna Dostoevsky

Finding and accepting our strength is a very important aspect of knowing ourselves as women. Adolescents do not usually know their own strength, but women do. When we deny our strength, we give up pieces of who *we* are. When we use our strength for power over others, we deny who *they* are. Either way, we lose.

Much of our strength comes from knowing and accepting ourselves and accepting that we are not the center of the universe. As we accept ourselves, we come to realize that our strength is directly connected with and one with a power greater than ourselves. When we tap into that power, we know that we have all the strength we need for whatever comes.

———

AS THE OLD *Ethiopian proverb states, "When spider webs unite, they can tie up a lion."*

SELF-CONFIDENCE

Class is an aura of confidence that is being sure without being cocky. Class has nothing to do with money. Class never runs scared. It is self-discipline and self-knowledge. It's the sure-footedness that comes with having proved you can meet life.

—Ann Landers

Self-confidence is so relaxing. There is no strain or stress when one is self-confident. Our lack of self-confidence mostly comes from trying to be someone we aren't. No wonder we do not feel confident when we are living a lie. When we realize that the best we have to bring to any situation is being just who we are, we relax. People who are cocky often show an alarming lack of self-confidence. They don't know what they have to offer. When we know what we have to offer and we bring it to each situation, that's all we need to do.

———————————

I LIKE *being a classy woman. No show . . . no blow . . . just the facts.*

HOLIDAYS/FRANTIC

Holidays and frantic aren't necessarily synonymous.
—Anne Wilson Schaef

We see the holiday season coming and we immediately feel exhausted and overwhelmed. We have to maintain our usual workday and, in addition, shop for gifts, decorate the house, do the extra holiday baking, attend additional social functions, and look great. For some of us, "the season to be jolly" becomes the season to wipe ourselves out. As women who do too much, we have come to dread the holiday season.

This is a good year for us to stop, take stock, and see what is really important for us this season. Perhaps we love the traditions. Which ones can we continue and be healthy? Perhaps we can try asking for help and stop trying to do everything ourselves. This season we have the opportunity to let ourselves feel the meaning of peace—peace within and peace with the world.

———————

DOING THE HOLIDAY SEASON *sanely is part of my healing process. I have that opportunity this season. Ho ho ho.*

HEALING

I will tell you what I have learned myself. For me, a long five- or six-mile walk helps. And one must go alone and every day.

—Brenda Ueland

Healing takes time. Healing is an every day affair. Some traumatic events in our lives require physical, emotional, and/or spiritual healing, and sometimes we just need to let the nicks, chips, and dents from everyday living heal. Doing the work we do and holding things together the way we do takes its toll.

When we need these healing times, there is nothing better than a good long walk. It is amazing how the rhythmic movements of the feet and legs are so intimately attached to cobweb cleaners in the brain. And we must take a *long* walk, because at first we think about our problems. These thoughts dissipate over time, thus allowing the healing to begin and we are less focused on our thinking.

WHEN MY HEELS *touch the earth, I am healing my wounds.*

LOVE

We can only learn to love by loving.
—Doris Murdock

Many women who do too much believe that there are tricks to loving. If we can just look sexy enough, we can make others love us. Or if we just take care of others and make ourselves indispensable, they will love us. We don't learn to love by loving, we try to control love by manipulation. Unfortunately, these methods do not teach us much about loving.

Loving is a risk. It is letting go of expectations and just allowing. Some of us doubt our capacity to love because we have been raised in dysfunctional families and never really have had much experience of clear loving.

Loving always had strings attached or demands that we had to meet. Hence we have practiced loving as we learned it in our families.

Fortunately, we are capable of new learning. And it starts right inside of us. When we experience loving ourselves, we begin to learn by loving.

———————

AS I LOVE MYSELF, *it is only a short step to the loving of others.*

December 19

COMMUNICATION

*If you have anything to tell me of importance, for
God's sake begin at the end.*
                                    —Sarah Jeanette Duncan

Women have always believed that the goal of communication is to bridge, connect, clarify, and facilitate
understanding. We have often developed this skill and
been good communicators.

Then we find that in our worklives, communication
is used in quite different ways than we had realized.
Communication is used to manipulate, control, confuse, and intimidate—to create barriers rather than
to bridge them. Success is intimately linked with this
confusing and confounding form of communication.
We are told that we have to play the game.

Later we find that the people we admire often are
very direct and refuse to play the game. We have been
tempted to abandon our communication skills, and
we sorely need them.

BEGINNING *at the end may be a good start. At least
it's more direct.*

JOYFULNESS

Surely the strange beauty of the world must somewhere rest on pure joy!

—Louise Bogan

Indeed, the world is so beautiful . . . and so imaginative. Who would have thought to design a tree such that its limbs, when they become too heavy, send down another trunk, so that a single tree repeating this process many times over can eventually cover an area the size of an entire block? Imagine a tree that is so tall that we can't really see the top—a tree that has developed at least three methods of reproducing itself so as not to become extinct? Indeed, "the strange beauty of the world must somewhere rest on pure joy." We have the opportunity to experience that joy. When we notice, the strange beauty of the earth is all around us.

IT PROBABLY WON'T HURT *to give thanks that the design and creation of the world was not left in our hands.*

December 21

INSPIRATION

Inspiration comes very slowly and quietly.
— Brenda Ueland

Sometimes we forget that to do our work well, whatever it is, we must have inspiration. This is true for any work, no matter how menial it may seem. Inspiration is the gentle listening to the wisdom of our inner being.

Brenda Ueland said that it comes slowly and quietly. I might also add that it comes when it wishes and not on demand. Like any process, we cannot force it. We must wait with it.

How sad that we have relegated inspiration to poets, artists, and writers! How sad that we cannot see that good child-rearing requires inspiration, that good management requires inspiration, regardless of the task. When we take away the possibility of our own inspiration, we relegate ourselves to a tedious existence. Inspiration adds spice and zest to our lives and allows them to be lives, not existences.

———————

WHEN I WAIT *with inspiration, my time is not wasted.*

December 22

CHOICES/FEAR/CHANGE

Change really becomes a necessity when we try not to do it.

—Anne Wilson Schaef

Risk and fear—we will do anything to avoid them both. Where did we get the idea that it is bad to feel fear and that we cannot handle our fear? We will do anything to avoid the fear of making a choice. We have another baby, or take on more work, or get busy with a new project around the house—anything.

We have so much fear of facing ourselves and confronting the choices we need to make that we are willing to wreck our lives and the lives of those around us in order not to have to make a choice.

We always resent it when others make decisions for us, *and* we do not want to be responsible for our choices. If we can manage to get someone else to make a choice for us, then we do not have to own the consequences.

I SAY *I want to be my own person, and sometimes that scares me to death. . . . That's OK.*

December 23

FEAR/CONTROL

Fear has a smell, as love does.
                                        —Margaret Atwood

The tightening of the stomach, the sweaty palms, the increasing inability to focus, the tingling in our arms and hands, and the anxiety about looking good or having the right answer—we all know about fear.

Unfortunately, the life of the woman who does too much is controlled by fear. What if we're not good enough? What if we're not on time? What if nobody likes us? By the time we have worked ourselves up into a lather, we are incapable of producing anything good. Fear and our illusion of control are intimately related. It is when we believe that we can control the outcome and the responses of others that we get fearful. Our worrying is a form of pre-control.

———————————

AS I ACKNOWLEDGE *my fear and turn it over to a power beyond myself, I can get the job done and done well.*

Causes/Dualism

> *The main dangers in this life are the people who want to change everything . . . or nothing.*
>
> —Lady Astor

How aptly put! Lady Astor put her finger on the meaning of dualism and the horror of being caught in a dualism. Those who want to change everything often become ruthless in their laser focus upon what they know is right.

Those who want to change nothing have become so enured to themselves and other beings that they only pass through life not looking to the right or to the left. Neither group does much for itself or anyone else. Actually, both groups operate out of the same self-centered focus.

What is the third option? The third option is to be present to ourselves and others, accepting those things which we cannot change, changing the things we can, and knowing the difference.

WHEN I *get caught up in a "cause," I become the problem. When I do nothing about the world in which I live, I am the problem.*

December 25

CONNECTEDNESS

God knows no distance.
                              —Charleszetta Waddles

How far away we seem at times from any Higher Power. We simply cannot connect with a power greater than ourselves, and we lose faith in its existence.

It is important to remember that the distance is within *us*. We are the ones who have moved away from that power and that connectedness. It has not moved away from us.

Our rushing around, our busyness, our constant caretaking and compulsive working leave little or no time or energy for anyone or anything to enter. Yet when we stop and notice, the connection with this power greater than ourselves is always there. It has never left us. *We* have left us.

———————————

THE DISTANCE *is mine. The potential for connectedness is mine, also.*

December 26

GROWTH

Lying, walking, sitting in this room, she felt herself ripening and coloring.

—Meridel Le Sueur

We have such a cult of youth in this society that, for a woman, growing older is a terrifying experience. Meridel Le Sueur's usage of the words "ripening" and "coloring" are very soothing. If I see myself ripening and becoming richer as I grow older, if I see myself developing a more intricate patina, my process of growth takes on a different tone.

We have two big dogs in our household, a seven-year-old Great Dane queen (seven is old for a Great Dane!) and a happy tramp-like German shepherd about two years old. Although she is busy being a queen, and he is busy growing up, they have the most beautiful, devoted, and caring relationship. He does not seem to mind that she is an "old lady" and has some grey hair. As I watch them, I realize that human beings are probably the only species that worship youth and disdain maturity. Among animals, it just doesn't seem to matter.

I COULD NOT KNOW *what I know today if I weren't the age I am. I have the continual opportunity to grow.*

PROCRASTINATION: STEP ONE

When I keep putting something off, it may not be pro-crastination, but a decision I've already made and not yet admitted to myself.

—Judith M. Knowlton

Contrary to popular belief, we workaholics are not women who are constantly doing something. We are often too busy and overworked, so that many times we just collapse into a morass of procrastination. We know that we have things that need to be done, and the more we think about them, the more leaden we feel. Sometimes it seems that we just cannot get our bodies out of bed, lift our arms, or hold a pen. We just cannot *make* ourselves do any more. Of course, when this lethargy takes over, we can sink into black periods of self-castigation.

At such times, it is important to remember that procrastinating is part of our disease and that we are powerless over this disease. It is only when we admit this powerlessness, acknowledge that we become in-sane with our procrastination, see that a power greater than ourselves can restore us to sanity, and turn our life and will over to that power, that we may, indeed, see that we have made a decision and can admit this decision to ourselves.

I CERTAINLY DO *make my life complicated some-times. Fortunately, there is another way.*

December 28

CLARITY/CHANGES/GROWTH

*Then I began to realize that I had to take another step
in my evolution and growth.*

—Eileen Caddy

We sometimes avoid getting clear because we intuitively know that when we get clear we will have to
make some changes in our lives. We are so accustomed to doing what is expected of us that it is difficult to know what we want or need. We can so easily
give in to the demands of others, especially if they are
in positions of authority, that we find ourselves confused and lacking clarity.

In spite of our confusion, our inner process continues to push us toward our evolution and growth. Something in us struggles for clarity.

———————————

GROWTH *and evolution are like breathing and eating . . . natural and intimately part of being human.*

AWARENESS OF PROCESS

Fate keeps happening.

—Anita Loos

Our lives are not set in stone. Lives, like flowers, continue to unfold. We have options and we have choices all along the way.

Certainly we have been influenced by our past and the many forces that have impinged upon us in our formative years. Yet we do have the ability to alter our present and our future.

Fate is a process that continues to emerge. As we accept who we are, we have the possibility of becoming someone else. That is the paradox of life and of living.

When I can let life happen, I feel better. When I can participate in the happening of my life, I soar.

––––––––––––

LIFE IS *in the living. The process of life keeps happening.*

December 30

COMPASSION/LOVING

Nobody has ever measured, even poets, how much the heart can hold.

—Zelda Fitzgerald

Some of us have become estranged from our feelings of compassion and love. We have believed that we had to become so tough and that we had to keep so busy that love and compassion became luxuries we could ill afford. Surely we could maintain our humanness with a few tax-deductible checks to the proper charities at the end of the year!

Yet, we know down deep that we are loving, compassionate women. When we give ourselves time, we care about people, and there are many things we love about our lives. Our hearts have a limitless capacity for caring and compassion.

TO LET MY HEART *swell with feelings of love and compassion is better than any combination of vitamins and exercise I could ever devise.*

BEAUTY

Happily may I walk.
May it be beautiful before me.
May it be beautiful behind me.
May it be beautiful below me.
May it be beautiful above me.
May it be beautiful all around me.
In beauty it is finished.

—Navajo prayer

If one reads this prayer very slowly, one feels its immensely profound simplicity. Imagine ourselves surrounded by beauty! When we think of being surrounded by beauty, we think of some island paradise or Shangri-la.

Yet, when we read this poem slowly, we begin to realize that we *are* surrounded by beauty! We see that this prayer is not only a request, it is simultaneously a statement of fact.

My life does have elements of beauty before, behind, below, and above me. I am surrounded by beauty.

WHEW! *Beauty is in the eye of the beholder!*

CREATIVITY/ALONE TIME

I can always be distracted by love, but eventually I get horny for my creativity.

—Gilda Radner

Nothing can replace creativity in our lives—not work, not love, not children, nothing. We may be creative in all these areas, yet our creative impulses must find their own avenue for expression.

Regardless of how interesting and challenging our work is and how creative we are with our work, we need times of quiet reflection to tap into the deep recesses of our being and see what is perking there. There is no substitute for our creativity, which is usually tapped when we are alone.

———————————

I LIKE *the way Gilda Radner puts it: "Eventually I get horny for my creativity."*

CONFUSION

*It was an immense betrayal—the more terrible because
he [she] could not grasp what had been betrayed.*
—Ayn Rand

One of the primary characteristics of the addictive
process is confusion. We are told that we should be
logical and rational, and so we try to be. Yet so many
of the things that happen to us just don't make any
sense. We become confused and frustrated, and we
try harder to understand. We believe that if we can
just understand what is happening we will feel better
and we can then handle the situation.

In our recovery we have learned that when any person or group is functioning addictively, nothing makes
sense. We can't understand what is going on because
it's insane. It's not understandable.

———————————————

WHEN *something is not understandable, it is best to
turn it over to a Higher Power and move on.*

Perfectionism/Procrastination

I know if I do it just one more time, I can get it right.
—Anonymous

And one more time, and one more time, and one more time. Perfectionism is a difficult and impossible task master. Also, perfectionism is a way of defining the task and ourselves from outside and may have nothing to do with what the task really is or who we really are.

In fact, we may use perfectionism to keep ourselves from getting anything done. If it has to be done perfectly, why even start? Perfectionism and procrastination go hand in hand, and accomplish nothing.

We need to remember that we are doing the task at hand and therefore what we have to bring to the task is ourselves, our accumulated knowledge and experience, and our creativity. Who could ask for anything more?

LET ME NOT ASK *for anything more today than to bring what I have to each task at hand.*

HONESTY

*But I don't let the cold feeling stay there because, just
the same . . . I know that what I say is true, because it
is true to me and therefore I say it freely and you must
have it.*

—Brenda Ueland

If something is true for us, we must trust that truth.
We live in a society that is built on dishonesty and am-
biguity. In some business and political circles, the
"good communicator" is the one who can intimidate,
confuse, confound, and *win*. The art of clear, honest
communication sometimes seems to have disappeared
with the age of innocence.

But somewhere down deep inside each of us is a
longing to be honest, to say what is true for us and
speak it freely, letting others have it. We live in a society that is shriveling up from the lack of honesty. We
are shriveling up from the lack of honesty. Our honesty is essential for our recovery.

———————

WE HAVE BEEN TAUGHT *to be afraid of our honesty. Yet it is the key to breaking down denial and the
door to healing.*

TRUST

Believing in our hearts that who we are is enough is the key to a more satisfying and balanced life.
—Ellen Sue Stern

I am enough! I have always been afraid of being too much or too little. What a relief I feel when I just sit with the possibility that I am enough. Can it really be true that I am not what I do or what I produce or what I accomplish? What if I am enough and I accomplish what I want to do? Would that truly be enough? Probably!

I would like a "satisfying and balanced" life. I would like more time and energy for my work, myself, and those I love. When I recognize that *I am enough,* I will have what I want and need.

I WILL SIT *with this feeling of being enough and let it be with me today.*

RELATIONSHIPS

Girls must be encouraged to go on [after college], to make a life plan. It has been shown that girls with this kind of commitment are less eager to rush into early marriage. . . . Most of them marry, of course, but on a much more mature basis. Their marriages then are not an escape but a commitment shared by two people that become part of their commitment to themselves and society.

—Betty Friedan

We don't know much about healthy relationships in this society. Most of our models for relationships are of addictive relationships, and we do those well. Too often we look to relationships as an external fix. We expect them to give us our identity and make our lives all right. When we do this, we bring no one to the relationship. We are like Jello, and we ask our partners to give us form by means of a relationship. Without the external mold of a relationship, the Jello dissolves into a puddle. Who wants to or even can relate to a puddle of Jello?

———————

IF I WANT *to be in a relationship, I have to bring someone to it . . . me.*

BEING TORN/GUILT

No woman should be shamefaced in attempting, through her work, to give back to the world a portion of its heart.

—Louise Bogan

It is difficult for women to do our own work. Women artists are frequently expected to keep house, run a family, do the carpool, cook all the meals, do the cleaning, and be able to spend their "spare" moments in their (usually makeshift) studio with their work. Life is never easy for an artist in this culture. Life is almost impossible for a woman artist in this culture.

But women artists are not alone in this struggle. Any woman who does too much cannot help but see the effect of her addiction on her family. Even when we firmly believe that our work should come first, we feel terrible pangs of guilt when our spouses and children have to make appointments with us to see us at all.

———————

A WORKING WOMAN *is one of the best balancing acts in this three-ring circus we call life. At least we are not alone in struggling with this issue.*

CREATIVITY

They say the moon is feminine. What will happen to me if I bathe myself in the creative feminine?
— Michelle

I like the image of the moonlight acting as an activator to help the emergence of what is already there within me!

If I bathe myself in moonlight, what miraculous and surprising images might emerge?

I suppose the real issue is not the magic of the moonlight, but whether I am willing to slow down enough to let any form of nature have an opportunity to bathe me.

Ancient peoples knew that connecting with nature released curative and creative energies. I, too, need nature in my life.

GETTING in nature may not be easy and even cities have moonlight.

GIFTS/CONTROL/RIGIDITY/ STUBBORNNESS

We don't make mistakes. We just have learnings.
—Anne Wilson Schaef

When we look at how our fear of making mistakes has deprived us of many of the most important issues of our lives, we give thanks that we no longer have to be so fearful of doing something wrong.

Life gives us many opportunities to learn the lessons we need to learn. Our inner beings are very conservation minded—they recycle our experience until we learn the lesson we need to learn.

The cost of the personal tuition that we have to pay is directly proportionate to our stubbornness and rigidity. The more stubborn and rigid we are, the harder we have to get hit alongside the head in order to learn. If we do not learn from our mistakes the first time, we'll get another chance . . . and another . . . and another.

———————

I GIVE THANKS *for my opportunities to learn, even if they don't always look like gifts at the time.*

CREATIVITY

Why should we all use our creative power? . . . Because there is nothing that makes people so generous, joyful, lively, bold and compassionate, so indifferent to fighting and the accumulation of objects and money.
—Brenda Ueland

So much of our frustration and irritability is a reaction to not using our creative powers. All of us have areas of creativity, and each of us has a unique creativity that is especially related to our talents and personality. Whenever we look at others and think, "I can't paint like that," or "I don't have the talent she does," we move a step further away from realizing what *we* have.

When we block our creativity, we lose touch with our joy and our liveliness. Is it any wonder that we become cantankerous and try to fill up the loneliness for our creative selves with money and things—which never quite do the job.

––––––––––––––

WHAT I REALLY *search for is me, and I am by nature creative.*

HOUSEWORK

*Cleaning your house while your kids are still growing
is like shoveling the walk before it stops snowing.*
—Phyllis Diller

I never understand why housework is not added to
the list of inevitables like taxes and death. No matter
what we are trying to get done or how much we need
a rest, etc., housework is always calling to us like the
siren's song: "Come do me . . . come do me." I have
thought of inventing a birth control spray that pre-
vents the housework from reproducing itself while
we sleep. When we get up in the morning there always seems to be more housework than when we
went to bed.

The nice thing about housework, of course, is that
it doesn't go away. We can go ahead and do some of
our creative work or soak in the tub, and it will be
there waiting when we come back to it.

SINCE HOUSEWORK *is always there waiting for
me, I might as well go ahead and do what I want.*

ACTION/CONTROL

*I have always had a dread of becoming a passenger in
life.*

—Princess Margrethe of Denmark

As women, we have been raised to expect someone to
take care of us. Most professional women prize our
independence. Yet down deep we often have a secret
wish that someone else would take responsibility for
our lives. Frequently we vacillate between wishing to
be passengers in life and asserting that we can handle
things ourselves. Sometimes we get stuck between
these two polarities. We believe that we must either
resign ourselves to going along for the ride or we
must be in the engine running the train. We do not
see the third option—take responsibility for our lives
and simultaneously turn them over to a power greater
than ourselves.

To participate in our lives does not mean that we
control our lives. Not to control our lives does not
mean that we are passive.

———————————

I DO NOT NEED *to choose between being a passenger or being an engineer. I can live my process.*

HONESTY/HONORING ONESELF

How many are silenced, how many women never "find their voice" because in order to get to their art they would have to scream?

—Ann Clark

Some of us find the words "obligations to myself" foreign. We have been raised to believe that we should sacrifice ourselves in order to be good. Then others of us have reacted to the female cult of self-sacrifice and decided that we needed to be selfish and to focus upon ourselves. Often we bounce back and forth between these two choices. Unfortunately (or fortunately, as the case may be), neither is satisfactory. Either way, we feel lonely, at loose ends, and unfulfilled.

The third option is to *honor* ourselves. When we honor ourselves and give out of that honoring, our giving is very clean. If we are not honoring ourselves, our giving has strings attached and is uncomfortable for the giver and the receiver.

WHEN I HONOR *myself, I discover the magic of my voice and my productions.*

IMPRESSION MANAGEMENT

We will discover the nature of our particular genius when we stop trying to conform to our own or to other people's models, learn to be ourselves, and allow our natural channel to open.

—Shakti Gawain

Impression management is trying to control how others see us. It is a subtle form of control and comes out of our feelings of insecurity, fear, and vulnerability. Impression management is exhausting and time-consuming. Impression management keeps us so busy trying to please and trying to keep ourselves safe that it completely keeps us away from the nature of our "own genius."

Impression management has become a way of life for the contemporary professional woman. And she is not the only woman who specializes in impression management. Any woman who is out of touch with herself believes she has to control the perceptions of others. Therefore, she never really takes the risk of being known.

———————

WHEN WE TRY *to manage, we try to control. When we are ourselves, we can genuinely be* with *others.*

DEMANDING TOO MUCH

*To dream of the person you would like to be is to waste
the person you are.*

—Anonymous

We had so many dreams about the person we wanted
to be that we never had the time to be the women we
were. It is exciting to look back at our growth and see
that there is an intimate relationship between our no
longer trying to be someone and our beginning to be
who we are. We used to demand so much of ourselves. We have, in the past, tried to mold ourselves
into persons who had nothing in common with our
real selves, because we were fearful that our true
selves would never be enough.

Our Twelve-Step work has helped us to see that demanding too much of ourselves is part of the disease
and will dissipate as we work on our recovery.

———————————

ENOUGH OR NOT—*I'm all I've got—if you in-
clude my Higher Power.*

FREEDOM

Freedom means choosing your burden.
                              —Hephzibah Menuhin

No one has complete freedom. Complete freedom is a myth that is terrifying to most and a dream-filled illusion for others. While we are wrestling with our terror of complete freedom or fighting the constrictions in our lives, we forget the freedoms we already have. We have the freedom to choose our burdens.

Women who have no children have chosen the burden of full-time work *without* the freedom that relating to children brings. Women who have chosen to have children have chosen the burden of rearing children (and often full-time work out of the home also!). Whatever our choices, we have made them. They are ours. We have the freedom to live with them.

I HAVE CHOSEN *my burdens. Sometimes I don't see the freedom in that.*

INDEX